Value Based Education in Society and Holistic Approach in Education

About *Dev Sanskriti Vishwavidyalaya, Hardwar*

Dev Sanskriti Vishwavidyalaya, Hardwar came into existence on 23 May, 1999. His Excellency, the Governor of Uttarakhand State formalized it *through an Ordinance on 22 January, 2002. Dev Sanskriti Vishwavidyalaya is fundamentally different from existing other Universities of the world in respect of approach towards education. The objectives and activities of existing universitites are normally confined to academics. Here education endeavours to touch the spiritual, cultural, and social aspects of life. Its value based education contributed to a holistic personality development of students rather than just being the mode for providing them with skills to earn livelihood. It will further facilitate the emergence of divinity in students and provide opportunities for the efflorescence of their latent potential. The University is committed to the upliftment of both the Rishibhoomi Uttarakhand and Devbhoomi Bharat.*

The Dev Sanskriti Vishwavidyalaya is managed by Shantikunj, through Ved Mata Gayatri Trust. Impressed by the altruistic activities of Shantikunj. It is everyone's aspiration that Dev Sanskriti Vishwavidyalaya should be a university with a difference. The planners want it to be a place where social, national and global welfare can be effectively nurtured.

Value Based Education in Society and Holistic Approach in Education

Editors
Dr. Jyotsna Saxena
Dr. R.P. Karmyogi
Dr. Y.K. Gupta

Dev Sanskriti Vishwavidyalaya Hardwar
&
Indian Association of Teacher Educators
In Association with
Anamika Publishers & Distributors (P) Ltd.

ANAMIKA PUBLISHERS & DISTRIBUTORS (P)LTD.
4697/3, 21A, Ansari Road, Daryaganj, New Delhi 110002
Phone: 2328 1655, 23270239; Fax . : 011-27868035
E-mali : anamikapublishers@yahoo.co.in

First Published 2009

ISBN 978-81-7975-294-4

PRINTED IN INDIA

Published by Anamika Publishers & Distributors (P) Ltd., 4697/3, 21A, Ansari Road, Daryaganj, New Delhi 110002. Typeset by Nidhi Laser Point, Delhi and Printed at Nagri Printers, Delhi.

Our Contributors

1. Miss. Anju Sharma, D.W.T. (P.G.) College, Dehradun.
2. Anurag Bhatnagar, Research Scholar, K.G.K. College, Moradabad, Presently working as Lecturer in Psychology.
3. Dr. Asha Sharma, Lecturer, Department of Education, Mahatma Gandhi Gramoday Vishwavidyalaya, Chitrakoot, Satna.
4. B.K. Savitri Bahen, Brahma Kumari Academy for a Better World, Gyan Sarovar, Maunt Abu (Raj.).
5. Dr. B.P. Uniyal, Education Department, Tehri Campus, H.N.B. Garhwal University, Srinagar.
6. Dr. B.R. Kukreti, Reader, IASE Rohilkhand University, Bareilly.
7. Dr. Bhopal Singh, Professor, IASE Deemed University, Sardar Shahr, (Raj.)
8. Ms. Bimla Verma, Ex-Principal, D.W.T. (P.G.) College.
9. Dr. C.S. Shukla, Head, Deptt. of Teacher Education, Vardhman (P.G.) College, Bijnor.
10. Mrs. Geetika Mehrotra, Lecturer, D.W.T. (P.G.) College Dehradun. Presently working as HOD in Dronas institute of Education.
11. Mrs. Gurpreet Randhawa, Research Scholar.
12. Gyanendra Nath Tiwari, Deptt. of Education, University of Allahabad.
13. Dr. H.S. Randhawa, Reader in English, D.A.V. (P.G.) College.
14. Dr. J.K. Joshi, Professor and Dean, Faculty of Education, S.S.J. Campus, Kumaon University, Almora.
15. Dr. Jyotsna Saxena, Reader D.W.T. (P.G.) College, Dehradun.
16. Dr. Kusum Lata Rathor, Reader, H.K.M., Sitapur.
17. Dr. L. Rawat, Principal, D.W.T. (P.G.) College, Dehradun.
18. Mrs. Manju Rani, Lecturer, Asian School, Dehradun. Presently working in Trinity College of Education.
19. Manoj Kumar Saxena, Lecturer, BVMTT, College, Banswara (Raj.)
20. Ms. Mudita Bhatnagar, Deptt. of Education, B.S.A. College, Mathura.
21. Dr. (Mrs.) N. Shamshi, Head Mistress, Asian School, Dehradun.
22. Dr. Navneet Arora, Mechanical and Industrial Engineering

Department, I.I.T. Roorkee.

23. Dr. P. Ananda, Programme Officer, DEP-DPEP, IGNOU, New Delhi.
24. Ms. Payal Khanna, Lecturer, Deptt. of Psychology, Dayanand Degree College, Moradabad.
25. Dr. Purnima Srivastava, Head, Deptt. of Education, K.L.D.A.V. College, Roorkee.
26. R.C. Nautiyal, Professor and Former Dean, Department of Education, Tehri Campus, H.N.B. Garhwal University, Srinagar.
27. Dr. R.P. Pathak, Reader in Education, L.B.S. Vidyapeeth, New Delhi.
28. Dr. Rachna Verma Mohan, Lecturer, S.L.B.S.R.S. Vidyapeeth, Deemed University, New delhi.
29. Dr. Rambha Joshi, Reader, Faculty of Education, S.S.J. Campus, Kumaon University, Almora.
30. Smt. Reena Saxena, Deptt. of Education, B.S.A. College, Mathura
31. Mrs. Ritu Garg. D.W.T. (P.G.) College, Dehradun.
32. Mr. S.K. Joshi, Deptt. of Teacher Education, Vardhman (P.G.) College, Bijnor.
33. Prof. S.P. Ahluwalia, Visiting Professor of Education.
34. Dr. S.S. Srivastava, Director, Bhartiya Siksha Shodh Sansthan, Lucknow, Former Dean of Education, BHU, Varanasi.
35. Ms. Sandhya Gihar, Lecturer, BVMTT College, Banswara (Raj.)
36. Dr. Sapna Verma, Senior Lecturer, Deptt. of Psychology, Gokul Das Hindu Girls P.G. College, Moradabad.
37. Sapna Sharma, Lecturer, Faculty of Education, Banasthali Vidyapeeth.
38. Shireesh Pal Singh, Presently working as Lecturer in Education, S.G.R.R. (P.G.) College, Dehradun.
39. Vijaishri Bhati, Lecturer, Amity Institute of Education, Saket, New Delhi.

Preface

Education is a process of human enlightenment and empowerment for the achievement of better and higher quality of life. A teacher's role in a society is one of the tremendous responsibility and importance. Enlightened, emancipated and empowered teacher lead communities and nation in their march towards better and higher quality of life. The teacher plays a vital role in shaping the personlity of his students, that leaves an indelible impression on their right way. An impressive and real teacher leads multitudes of childrens on path of enrichment and progress.

According to Ryans—"A teacher is effective to the extent he is able to develop basic skills, understanding about the world around work habits, desirable attitudes, value judgement and adequate personal adjustment of the pupil."

There is no denial regarding the importance of teacher in the development of any society. Like wise the role of the teacher in building of a society and thereby the nation has been highlighted by all education commmissions and committees. A teacher must succeed in conveying the larger ideals of service to the community. He is to teach the importance of character, integrity, discipline and value of humanism to his pupils, so that our educational institutions become and nurseries, not only of good students but of good citizens as well.

In this book we have made an attempt to collect ideas and views of educationists on a very important aspect of education that is value based education and holistic development ... the merit of this book lies in the contemporary relevance of the subject and a wide variety of topics covered in this volume. It is a matter of immense personal gratification that the distinguished academicians and scholars from all over the country have contributed their enriched thought in this book.

They have contributed their wisdom in a logically arranged sequence and explained the theoritical and practical aspects of value education.

We believe that the book will be immensely significant and useful for researchers and academicians and it will contribute in professional development of teachers in reference to value base education and holistic approach in education.

In this book total twenty four papers spread over many areas of value education. All contributors deserve our appreciation for their scholarly presentation in producing this book.

We are grateful to Dev Sanskriti Vishwavidyalaya, Hardwar which has inspired us to bring out this issue of book for the benefit of entire society of scholars, the character builders of the masses.

Editors

प्राक्कथन

एक समय था जब प्राचीन भारत में शिक्षा का अर्थ था – 'जीवन की तैयारी'। तब गुरुकुलों और आरण्यकों में ऋषियों के सतत सान्निध्य में पढ़ते-पढ़ते छात्रों में ज्ञान एवं गुण का ऐसा समुच्चय विनिर्मित होता था, जिससे सहज ही व्यवहार में अपेक्षित परिवर्तन मूर्तिमान हो उठता था। इसमें अहम भूमिका निभाती थी — आचार्यों के जीवन की प्रामाणिकता। तब जीवन मूल्यों के विकास के लिए न तो कोई शिविर लगाने पड़ते थे न पृथक से कोई संगोष्ठियाँ ही आयोजित करनी पड़ती थीं। ऐसा इसलिए था कि जीवन मूल्य अध्ययन-अध्यापन में ही घुले-मिले रहते थे और तब व्यक्तिगत जीवन, सामाजिक जीवन की तैयारी होता था। इस प्रक्रिया में मूल्य परोक्ष रूप से स्वतः ही समाज में घुल-मिल जाते थे।

अब व्यक्ति का जीवन भौतिकवाद से ओतप्रोत है। इसके भौतिकवादी चिन्तन ने न केवल दृष्टिकोण ही बदला है, बल्कि भारतीय शिक्षा का स्वरूप ही बदल दिया।

अब तो पढ़ने-रटने और पास होने में ही शिक्षा सिकुड़कर रह गई है। इस शिक्षा की संकुचित सीमा के कारण ही गुणों की उपेक्षा हुई, परिणामस्वरूप जीवन के प्रथम चरण से ही जीवन मूल्यों का ह्रास होना शुरू हुआ। इतिहास पर दृष्टिपात करें तो इस देश में पृथक से कहीं जीवन मूल्यों के विकास के लिए कोई औपचारिक प्रयास नहीं किए गए, बल्कि चिन्तन, चरित्र और व्यवहार का आनुषंगिक फल था—जीवन मूल्य।

आज स्थिति की विडम्बना यह है कि जीवन मूल्यों के ह्रास का सिलसिला कहीं थमता नजर नहीं आता। यहां तक कि पढ़े-लिखे मानव की शक्ल में भी दानव पनपता जा रहा है। इस भयावह स्थिति को देखकर सब तो मूक दर्शक बने नहीं रह सकते। समय-समय पर शिक्षा आयोगों ने भी इस पर गहरी

चिन्ता व्यक्त की है। राष्ट्रीय शिक्षा नीति 1986 में तो यह उल्लेख है कि 'जीवन मूल्यों का ह्रास तो ठीक है, पर इन मूल्यों पर से आस्था ही उठती जा रही है यह भारी चिन्ता का विषय है।' सुविज्ञ पाठक यह जानते हैं कि मूल्यों के विकास में प्रथम जिम्मेदारी अभिभावकों की है, पर ये अपनी जिम्मेदारी का कितना निर्वाह कर पाते हैं? आखिर नजर शिक्षक पर ही ठहरती है। अच्छा शिक्षक कब तक मौन रहेगा।

डा. (श्रीमती) ज्योत्स्ना सक्सेना, रीडर, दयानन्द शिक्षण महाविद्यालय, देहरादून ने जीवन मूल्यों की गिरावट पर भारी चिन्ता व्यक्त की और गहराई से विचार करते हुए मूल्यपरक शिक्षा को लक्ष्य करके नेशनल सेमिनार की पहल की। श्रीमती सक्सेना ने डा० प्रणव पद्या तथा I.A.T.E के सचिव डा० वाई०के० गुप्ता, प्रोफेसर प्रमोद भटनागर, शान्ति कुंज के परामर्श से ऐसी प्रभावी कार्ययोजना तैयार की जिससे देश में विभिन्न राज्यों के शिक्षा जगत से जुड़े लगभग दो सौ विद्वानों ने स्वप्रेरणा से इस सेमिनार में भागीदारी की। यहाँ यह बात उल्लेखनीय है कि इस अवसर पर जीवन मूल्यों से सम्बन्धित लगभग 159 पत्रों का अलग-अलग समूहों में वाचन हुआ। न केवल वाचन, बल्कि प्रत्येक पत्र ने विचार-विनिमय का ऐसा अवसर प्रदान किया जिसका मानव मूल्यों के विकास में निश्चित ही महत्वपूर्ण योगदान होगा।

जहाँ तक इस सेमिनार में पढ़े गए पत्रों का प्रश्न है इनमें मूल्यों को अनेक शीर्षकों में वर्गीकृत कर उनकी आवश्यकता और उपादेयता पर यथेष्ट सामग्री प्रस्तुत की गई है। इस विषयवस्तु में तथ्य और वे सुझाव सम्मिलित हैं जिनसे शरीर, मस्तिष्क और आत्मा के विकास की सम्भावनाएँ पुष्ट होंगी। पुस्तक में दिए गए कुछ विचार-बिन्दु अत्यधिक महत्वपूर्ण हैं, यथा– Symptoms of Morality, Guideline for Value Education Planning. इसके अन्तर्गत Self Oriented Value जिसमें तीस बिन्दुओं का समावेश किया गया है। Family Oriented Values भी है के अन्तर्गत 12 बिन्दुओं का समावेश है, Society Oriented Values में 18 बिन्दुओं का समावेश है और Nature Oriented Values के अन्तर्गत 12 बिन्दुओं का समावेश किया गया है। साथ ही इसमें पाठ्यक्रम निर्माण और शिक्षकों के उत्तरदायित्वों को भी निरूपित किया गया है और अभिभावकों को भी वह दिशा दी गई है, जिससे वे बच्चों

के निर्माण में अपनी सही भूमिका अदा कर सकें। (पृष्ठ 68–70) वस्तुतः इस पुस्तक में जीवन मूल्य और उनकी विकासात्मक प्रक्रियाओं को विशेषरूप से उभारा गया है। यह कहने में मुझे कोई संकोच नहीं है कि जीवन मूल्यों को आत्मसात करने की दृष्टि से मूल्यों के सैद्धान्तिक और व्यावहारिक पक्षों का अनोखा मणि–कांचन संयोग है।

मुझे विश्वास है कि आज मानव मूल्यों की गिरावट और जीवन की कसावट ने जो सांस्कृतिक विद्रूपता पैदा की है उसे सही दिशा देने और उसके रूप संवर्धन में निश्चित ही इस पुस्तक की अहम भूमिका होगी।

शांतिकुंज, हरिद्वार जहाँ यह सेमिनार आयोजित किया गया वहाँ की ऊर्जा निश्चित ही इस सेमिनार को सफल बनाने में सहयोगी रही। वहाँ की समुचित और सुचारू व्यवस्था सराहनीय रही, इसके लिए सभी ने आभार व्यक्त किया।

अन्त में इस नेशनल सेमिनार की संयोजिका डा०(श्रीमती) ज्योत्स्ना सक्सेना और संयोजक मण्डल के सभी विद्वान सदस्य तथा इस पुस्तक के विद्वान लेखकों, सम्पादकों को मेरा हार्दिक धन्यवाद।

डॉ. आर.पी. कर्मयोगी
कुलसचिव
देव संस्कृति विश्वविद्यालय
गायत्रीकुंज–शान्तिकुंज, हरिद्वार

Contents

1
Value: Bharatiya Point of View

S.S. Srivastava

"The expression "Value" chiefly has a commercial connotation and is not much connected to moral and ethical principle. Although the root of word "Value" might remotely have been drawn from "worthiness". But its common and direct usage is for 'rate' of 'the worth in terms of assets'. Therefore, "value can never be an eternal phenomenon. It is changeable in accordance with time, space, or utility. In ancient Indian canons, you will find such appropriate expressions as Dharma, Shila, Sadachara, Niti, etc. But the word "Mulya" is never found in our classical literature to convey the meaning of "Morality". In the English language too, there are many more appropriate expressions like morals, ethics, virteous conduct etc. But modern educationists have preferred to choose the word "Value" which is perhaps found more suitable by them as it is more closely related to the market language. The Indian imitators happily translate this as "Mulya" and talk about this in various levels of educational management. The most surprising matter is that the advocates of this "value-education" don't know of the nature of moral and ethical education. The basic misconception is the acceptance of knowledge as "Value neutral". Thus, they think you can put some values as an additional information like buttering your bread. They have not understood morality in its original sense. In their view, morality has nothing to do with tradition of spirituality or even with inner consciousness. Their conception of value is based at best on the principles of

Rationalism, Utilitarianism or Individualism. This view usually leads to making the issue of morality a matter of law and formal rules of do's and don'ts. Thereafter, everyone becomes dependent on law-enforcing agencies for moral of society". (Rinpoche, 2000)

Purushartha

However, in real sense of the term from Bharatiya point of view 'Value' may be taken as equivalent to "Purushartha" of Indian tradition, culture, psychology and philosophy. The concept of Purushartha is based on the realization that desires constitute the source of human action. The life of man centers around certain basic desires. Each of these desires or aspirations is distinct from the other in its object and each stimulates man to a particular mode of activity in order to satisfy it. Each individual, for example, has in him the sexual and parental urges, true of power and wealth, desire for the common good and hunger for communion with the unseen. These different activities react upon and modify one another. They function in interdependence in man's life. If life is considered as one whole then there is one master science of life, The purusharth, which recognizes its four supreme ends : Arth (wealth), Kama (physical-wellbeing), Dharma (righteousness) and Moksha (spiritual freedom).

The Purusharth have a gradation with each value constituting a preparatory stage for the realization of the succeeding one. Artha (the economic value) is only helpful as a means for satisfying one or the other diverse needs and desires of life. Their satisfaction is Kama (pleasure) which is not only physical but also psychological. Further, Artha and Kama are sought not only by man but by all living beings. They are the 'Values' which all living beings cherish. They are the 'Values' which all men are naturally inclined to seek, But the 'Value' of Dharma and Moksha are of a different nature and differentiate animal kingdom from the mankind.

The appeal of Dharma, which is moral value among the four 'Purusharthas' is exclusively restricted to 'Atman'. It determines what one ought to do in different life situations, in accordance with the best moral code. In this sense 'Dharma' acts as a regulating principle in life deciding between a right and a wrong Karma 'Dharma' furnishes the categorized into acceptable and unacceptable. As long as Dharma is not ignored, The pursuit and even enjoyment of Arth and Kama are not bad. Dharma, thus, helps one to discriminate between good and bad, and lead a good life, and herein lies its superiority over Artha and Kama.

But even higher than Dharma is Moksha, or spiritual bliss which is supreme happiness and therefore, the ultimate goal of human life, (Param Purushartha). So, Dharma, although good enough to be the goal of life in its own right, is to be considered as necessary stepping stone to the attainment of the supreme end of Moksha. That is a true transcendental self-realization and peaceful self-sufficiency.

Srivastava (1986) while elaborating the concept of self-realization writes. "There are in India two inter-related ideas that are centrally pertinent to education. These are the concept of "Swabhava" and "Swadharma".

'Swabhava' must not be confused by modern psychological term 'temperament', which refers to individual's, habit of preferences and of likes and dislikes, but it represents an expression emerging directly from the inner self, it is the becoming of the true soul (self or swa). The soul is the entity of delights, and its expressions are devoid of ignorance. To uncover this soul so that it may express its true nature more and more fully, is the real aim of human life and thus the real aim of education. It is through education that the individual has to recognize the true swabhava. Each individual has according to the profound wisdom of India, a unique function and a unique role to play in this vast universe. Each individual, thus, has an ideal function appropriate to his ideal nature and the law of that function, and the right step by which this law and this function can be developed and fulfilled is what is called for each individual, his own 'Swadharma'. 'Swadharma' may not be misconceived as 'religion' in modem sense of the term. It as not a prescription of a dogma or of commandment or of prescribed acts or rites or rituals. Swadharma is the inner law which has his own rhythm of development, his own cycle of development and his own line of development leading towards the fulfilment of right function and the role he has to fulfil in the world, to use the expression of Vedas, Swadharma is the individual expression of the 'Ritam' which is inalienable one with 'satyam' the truth and Supreme God.

REFERENCES

Chaudhary, H (1975), Yoga Psychology, London; Routledge and Keganpal.

Gita Press (1974), Srimad Bhagvadgita, Gorakhpur.

Rinpoche, S. (2000), Second Convocation Address of Faculty of Education, Banaras Hindu University, Varanasi.

Srivastava S.S. (1986), The Indian alternative : Education for peace and development. Paper presented and seminar-cum workshop on education and national development in 21st century, Faculty of Education, Banaras Hindu University.

2

Adolescents' Value Preferences to Some Psycho-Social Variables

Rambha Joshi
J.K. Joshi

Adolescence is a time of great possibility and it is also a time when most young people must pay a price for the privileges of growing-up. This time of great possibility as well as of 'privileges' and 'constraints' leads an individual to get himself engaged in:

(1) Forming, what Erikson (1971) has referred to as Ego-Identity.

(2) Acquiring and adhering to some values of a set of values prevailing in the society.

It may be argued that each individual gradually builds up a unique frame of reference—a set of basic assumptions concerning fact, possibility, and value—which provides him with a coherent picture of himself and his world. The formation of Ego-Identity and acquisition of and adherence to certain values may be assumed to depend mainly, along-with many psycho-social factors, on how adolescents perceive their home environment and school environment.

The need for a sense of identity is so vital and imperative that man could not remain sane if he did not find some way of satisfying it (Fromm, 1955:60). Putting together an identity has been assumed to be one of the major tasks of adolescence. To the adolescent the problem of his identity is basic one.

Adolescence is the time when the basic question, "Who am I?" is asked with unrelenting force and insistence and when reference groups, significant others, and available roles are most avidly scanned in an attempt to derive a more meaningful answer. Seeking an answer has been referred to as forming, what Erikson (1962) calls, an ego- identity—an image of himself which for the first time has consistency both in the way adolescent sees himself and the way others see him (Craig, 1976:407).

Conger (1977:516) has asserted that'....the problem of developing a strong sense of identity cannot be separated from the problem of values'. Rogers (1964) illustrated that adolescence is a potentially exciting time in the development of each individual's values.

In fact, it is within the confines of the family that adolescents hope to find the answer to the basis question 'who am I?' (Sebald, 1977:151). Furthermore, 'it remains important to remember, as Horrocks (1969) has suggested that the home is both status defining and experience-defining for the adolescent (Thornburg, 1975:123). School assumes a special role in the sense that' among the many environmental factors that may affect adolescents' views of themselves are those connected with school' (Jersild, et al., 1978:34).

Hence it was decided to understand adolescents' value preferences in relation to their ego- identity and their school and home environments.

Adolescents: Adolescents, here in this investigation, refers to a group of school-going male individuals, in the age-range of 13 to 19 years living in the hill areas of Kumaon Region.

Ego-Identity: Ego-identity, in the sense as it is employed in the present instigation has been first used by Erikson (1963) while presenting his model of the eight stages of human development which encompasses the entire of human life. In Erikson's view, every one experiences eight crises of conflicts in development and there are different points in the life cycle where specific developmental conflicts are paramount. The following shows the stage and its corresponding developmental conflicts:—

Stage	*Age*	*Conflict/Crisis*
1st stage	Birth to 1 year six months	Trust vs. Mistrust
2nd stage	2 to 3 year	Autonomy vs. Shame and doubt
3rd stage	4 to 5 year	Initiative vs. Guilt
4th stage	6 to 18 year	Industry vs. Inferiority
5th stage	12 to 18 year	Identity vs. Role Confusion
6th stage	19 to 25 year	Intimacy vs. Isolation
7th stage	26 to 65 year	Generativity vs. Self- absorption
8th stage	65 years onwards till death	Integrity vs. Despair

It is to be remembered that while each of Erikson's conflicts is critical at only one stage, it is present throughout the life.

To Erikson, ego- identity is the accrued confidence that the inner sameness and continuity are matched by the sameness and continuity of one's meaning for others.

In the present investigation an adapted and modified version of Ego-Identity Seale of Rasmussen (1964) has been used to measure the Ego identity of the adolescents. This scale contains six-dimensions corresponding to the six conflicts/ crises paramount at the first six-stages of life respectively.

Operationally, the term ego-identity may be said to be a trait of a variable measured by Ego-Identity Scale of Joshi (1984).

Values:

Havighurst (1972) sees one of the developmental tasks of adolescents as acquiring a philosophy of life: such a philosophy embodies the values which the individual holds to be of central importance to himself. This philosophy, organized around a hierarchy of values, serves as a reference point for the individual's behaviour.

Values may be thought of as emotional commitments to relevant group standards by which experiences and objects are judged and choices are made.

The dictionary definitions of the terms 'values' and 'value' are being given below:

(1) **'Values':** (Plural)' the qualities, customs, standards,

and principles of a people regarded as desirable. (The Living Webster Encyclopedic Dictionary of the English Language (1981), Delair Publishing Company I.N.C., Page 1093.)

(2) **'Value':** Any characteristic deemed important because of psychological, social, moral, or aesthetic considerations; commonly used in the plural, to refer to built-in inner systems of beliefs from which one can gain security of support'. (Dictionary of Education (1973) Ed. carter V. Good. McGraw Hill Book Company).

(3) Values are the pattern of preferences of generalised attitudes with (mostly) real independent existence indicating the desirability of behaviours in terms of Social, Moral, Aesthetical and Psychological needs. (S.P. Kulshrestha, Manual of Directions for Revised and Modified Hindi Adaptation of Study of Values, 1971, p. 4).

Kluckhohn (1954:395) defines value as "a conception, explicit or implicit, distinctive of an individual or characteristic of a group, of the desirable which influences the selection from available modes, means and ends of action."

Dacey (1979:358) refers values as 'the estimation of worth that person puts on all the various aspects of life.'

A psychological view of values offered by Ausubel and Sullivan is as below:–

Values refer to ways of striving, behaving and doing whenever purpose and direction are involved of choice and judgment are exercised. Values are implied in the relative importance an individual attaches to different objectives and activities, in his moral, social and religious beliefs and in his aesthetic preferences. They underlie sanctioned ways of behaving and interacting with people in a given culture and the kinds of personality traits that are idealised.

Operational Definition of Values:

In the present investigation Kulshrestha's 'Study of Values' test has been used for measuring values of the adolescents.

Hence the definition (iii) above may be treated as operational definition of values. Six values, namely Theoretical value, Economic Value, Aesthetic Value, Social Value, Political Value, and Religious Value are measured by this test.

This test is a revised and modified adaptation of the test entitled 'A Study of Values' by Allport, Vernon, and Lindzey (1960). The value types proposed by spranger (1928) form the basis for this well-known psychological test of Allport, Vernon and lindzey. Hence it seems important and worthwhile to present, in brief, the proposition of Spranger, so that an insight may be developed regarding what stands for the six values, namely Theoretical Value, Economic Value, Aesthetic Value, Political Value and Religious Value respectively.

Spranger (1928) contended that every person can be regarded as approaching - but rarely fitting perfectly within - one or more of six value types or value directions. In essence there seems to be six main types of values which appeal to people in varying degrees and around which they build the unity of their lives. These were described by Spranger in terms of pure of or "ideal" types of men.

1. **The Theoretical:** The primary value of the "Ideal" theoretical man is the discovery of truth. Since this involves the use of rational, critical, and empirical processes, the theoretical man is an intellectual-often a scientist or philosopher.
2. **The Economic:** The "Ideal" economic man values what is useful and is concerned with the business world of other practical affairs involving the production, marketing, or consumption of goods. Tangible wealth and material possessions are of central interest.
3. **The Aesthetic:** The "Ideal" aesthetic man sees his highest value in form and harmony. He may or may not be a creative artist, but he finds his chief interest in the artistic or aesthetic experiences in life. The aesthetic man views the economic or theoretical man as unappreciative of and destructive of aesthetic values.

4. **The Social:** The "Ideal" social man places great value on affiliation and love. The social man values other persons as individuals and tends to be kind and sympathetic. Often he views the theoretical and economic value orientations as cold and inhuman.
5. **The Political:** The "Ideal" political man places great value on power. His activities may not be restricted to the narrow range of politics. But his primary focus us in personal relationships is on power, influence, and active competition to maintain and expand his power.
6. **The Religious:** The highest value for the "Ideal" religious man may be called unity. He is mystical and seeks to comprehend and relate himself to the cosmos and to find higher level value experiences via his religious philosophy.

'This classification of values types has been criticized on the grounds that it does not exhaust the possibilities and that it provides an overly favourable view of man. For example, many people appear to have few if any strong values beyond those of hedonism and sensual pleasure. Also the six "Ideal" values types appear to represent nonexistent extremes and do not ordinarily exist in such perfect form in real life. Despite such limitations, however, these value orientations have the advantage of being amenable to measurement and help us understand the general directions that our value orientations may take.' (James C. Coleman, Psychology and Effective Behaviour: Bombay: D.B. Taraporevala Sons & Co. Pvt. Ltd. 1971, p. 439).

Study of Value Scale:

The test contains 45 questions/statements in two parts. Part I contains 30 questions/statements with two alternatives and part II contains 15 questions/statements with four alternatives. Students have to value them numerically.

It is a forced choice Instrument aims to measure the relative prominence of six basic interests or motives of personality. These are as follow:–

1. The Theoretical Value-refers to discovery of thought.
2. The Economic Value-refers to the utility or what is useful.
3. The Aesthetic Value-refers to the highest value in form and harmony.
   This is judged from the standpoint of Grace, Symmetry or Fitness.
4. The social value refers to love of people and sympathy.
5. The political value refers to the love power.
6. The religious value indicates the unity and oneness.

School Environment: SE, in this investigation, refers to the perception of adolescents of their school environment. Operationally, it may be said to be a variable measured by Home Environment Assessment Scale (HEAS) constructed and validated by Joshi (1984) for school-going male adolescents of hill areas of Kumaon Region.

Home Environment: HE, in this investigation refers to the perception of adolescents of their home environment. Operationally, it may be said to be a variable measured by Home Environment Assessment Scale (HEAS) constructed and validated by Joshi (1984) for school-going male adolescents of hill areas of Kumaon Region.

The sample consisted of 931 male adolescent students studying in classes IX to XII of Government Intermediate Colleges situated in the hill areas of Kumaon region. The following tools were employed to collect the relevant data:

1. Ego-identity Scale an adapted, modified and revalidated version of the Ego-identity Scale of Rasmussen (1964).
2. Study of Values Test of Kulshrestha (1971).
3. School Environment Assessment Scale (SEAS) of Joshi, J.K. (1984).
4. Home Environment Assessment Scale (HEAS) of Joshi, J.K. (1984).

Appropriate descriptive and inferential statistics were employed to attain the various objectives of the study. This statistical treatment of the data involved the computation of Pearson's, eta-coefficients and t-ratios. Factor Analysis

Technique was employed to extract some common factors as a result of constellation of various variables under investigation.

Conclusions: Some of the important conclusions of the study are as follows:

(1) The most preferred value of adolescents is Theoretical value and the least preferred value is Aesthetic value.

(2) With only slight exceptions, in general, the order of preference of various values of adolescents is as below:

(i) Theoretical Value
(ii) Social Value
(iii) Political Value
(iv) Religious Value
(v) Economic Value
(vi) Aesthetic Value

(3) During adolescence Economic Value, Political Value, Religious Values remain relatively stable and older adolescents (16 Years and above) are high on Theoretical Values and Social Values as compared to younger adolescents (13&14 years of age) but they are on Aesthetic value as compared to younger adolescents.

(4) The caste-hierarchical position does not seem to influence Theoretical value, Aesthetic value, Political value and Religious value of adolescents.

(5) More adherence to Economic Value and Social Value and less adherence to Aesthetic Value may lead an adolescent to form stable and stronger Ego-identify.

(6) Economic Value, Social Value and Religious Value are not related to school environment and home environment. Aesthetic Value is related negatively to school environment and home environment. Theoretical Value is not related to school environment but it bears a positive relationship with home environment. Reverse is true with Political value which is not related to home environment but it bears a positive relationship with school environment.

REFERENCES

Allport, G.W., Vernon, P.E. and Lindzey, G.A. Study of Values. Houghton Mifflin: BVoston, 1960.

Conger, J.J. Adolescence and Youth, Harper & Row: New York, 1977.

Craig, G.J. Human Development Prentice-Hall, Inc.: London, 1976.

Dacey, J.S. Adolescents Today, Goodyear Publishing Company Inc., California 1979.

Doctoral dissertation, Kumaon University, Nainital, 1984.

Erikson, E.H. Childhood and society Norton : New York, 1963.

Fromm, E. The Sane Society. Holt , Rinehart & Winston, New York, 1955.

Havighurst, R.J. Development Task and Education, David Mckay, New York, 1972.

Jersild, A.T. etal: The Psychology of Adobscence, MacMillan Publishing Co. In., New York, 1978.

Joshi J.K., Study of ego-identity and Value of Adolescence Living in Hill areas of Kumaon in relation to their School and Home Environment.

Kluckhohn, C., Values and Value Orientation in the theory of action. In T. Parsons and E.A. Shils (Eds.) Toward a General Theory of Action Harvard Univ. Pren : Cambridge. 1954.

Kulshreshtha, S.P. Manual of Direction for Revised and Modified Hindi Adapation of Study of Values. Rupa Phychological Corporation: Varanasi, 1971.

Mead, M. Coming of Age in Samoa, Morrow, New York. 1961.

Rasmussen, J.E. Relationship of ego-identity to Psychological effectivemen. Psychol. Rep. 1964, 15, 815, 825.

Sebald, H. Adolescence : A Social Psychological Analysis. Prentice hall, In., New Jersey, 1977.

Spronger, E. Lebeustorman (Translated : P. Pigore. Types of Men. Stac kert, New York. 1928.)

Thornbwrg. H.D. Development in Adolescence, Brooks Code Publishing Company, California, 1975.

3
Value Education and Current Issues

Jyotsna Saxena
Anju Sharma

Introduction

The dictionary defines the word "Value" as worth and it is further defined in the social sciences encyclopedia as interests, pleasure, likes, preferences, duties, moral obligations, desires, needs and wants. The word value is derived from the Latin word *"Valerie "which* means strong and vigorous. To be of value is to have certain virtues, a thing which is good. A wide accepted concept of value in traditional philosophy is "Truth, Goodness, Beauty", The "Satyam Shivam Sundaram". From the evolution of animal to man just gaining the human form did not make the man human. The human mind was also being developed intellectually and morally, leading to the attainment of power of thinking reasoning and capacity of thought along with certain qualities embedded into their character only then the true human was generated.

The values may be different according to the circumstances and situation of individuals. They have to be developed as internal instincts. These values form the base and foundation of the human being. They are the value of *rationality,* that is the recognition of the fact that existence exists, nothing can alter the truth and nothing can take precedence over the act of preceding it. The value of *independence,* the recognition of the fact that it is one's own responsibility to judge and nothing can help one escaping it. *Honesty,* the recognition of the fact that the unreal is unreal and can have no value, that neither love nor fame nor cash is a value of obtained by fraud. *Justice,* the recognition of the fact that one cannot fake the character of men as one cannot fake the character of nature, that one can judge all men as conscientiously as one judges inanimate objects with the same respect for truth , with the same incorruptible vision, by as pure and as rational a process of identification. *Pride,* The recognition of the fact that one is one's own highest value and like all of man's values it has to be earned.

Values and Current Situation

Today life around the globe is enriched with incredible technological advances. Every nation around the world is striving hard to bring into the lives of their citizens the marvels of science and technology. The development of communication and information technology has made the world a global village with improved interaction among the people of the world. Inspite of ever growing wonders of science and technology we are living in turbulent times, facing multi-dimensional hazards, which are beyond our imagination. Development strategies of various countries have brought about ethnic conflicts, nationalism and religious fanaticism. Never has one felt a need for more tolerance and peace, as the greed for material progress has brooked no limits. Deforestation, global warming, water and air pollution are consequences of industrial development making the earth more and more inhospitable. Finally, the advent of biotechnology and bio-informatics has on the one hand, increased agricultural production, improved medical facilities, but on the other hand has also created problems of 'gene cloning' and 'surrogate motherhood', hence raised complex ethical issues.

"The impact of ethics can be measured in high technology areas such as biology and medicine, as well as in the arcane vagaries of computerisation, a phenomenon which is affecting all spheres including private life. If we neglect to make a connection between basic ethics and technological progress, we would be ushering in an era of barbarism with a human face".

Human values are like valves in our personalities. When a

valve is operational in our being, it acts as like a safeguard. Each value is a safety valve just like in our heart. They operate to protect us from thoughts, words and arid actions that may otherwise have a detrimental effect when we are faced with crisis or conflicts. While the basic values of seeking the truth, practicing honesty and appreciating beauty, remain intact, secular values like tolerance, self-respect, love for human dignity, respect and compassion for others, individual freedom and human race. These problems are now assuming stronger forms and larger proportions. They are no longer individual or local, they are global affecting the whole mankind. In the world, moral and human values are declining to the point where man is capable of destroying not only himself but also the entire world.

The World Today and Value-crisis

This is an age of "Value-crisis". These words have been said over and over again by every individual on earth, half in fear that it is true and half in hope that the words have no meaning. Many observers feel that moral values are disintegrating in all walks of life, both public and personal. Indeed, 'Value-Crisis' is a global phenomenon of our times. Our growing progress in controlling the material world has not been matched by corresponding advances in human character and virtues. Who is to be blamed for the situation- none other than the world's moral code itself ! The sense of moral values has reached its climax a blind alley that is the end of its course.

Modern human life has become a personal projects, where each person through constant choices creates his or her own life. The concept of 'Values' is mystical of social. Since the supreme ideal is beyond the grasp of man's mind, he gives up eventually all ideals, all aspirations and all sense of his personal values. The vision, the mind, the self–noblest of all virtues is dead. Man realizes that he's incapable of what he had accepted as the noblest 'sacrifice', since virtue to the world consists of sacrifice. The world cursing human nature for its unwillingness to practice the virtues that have been demanded by it. It demands more and more sacrifices in the name of a return to morality, it has sacrificed justice to mercy, independence to unity, reason to faith, wealth to need, self-esteem to self-denial and happiness to duty.

Now that the world is a mirror of its own virtues and has achieved all that it held as good why does it shrink in horror form the sight of the product, images of its own virtues. Thus if in this age of moral crisis if man wishes to go on living what he needs is not to return to Morality - one thing which he has never known, but to discover it.

"Man has to be a man-by choice; he has to hold his life as a value –by choice; he has to learn to sustain it - by choice; he has to discover the values it requires and practice its virtues by choice."

—Ayn Rand.

Values Metamorphosis in the Education System

In the educational institutions the erosion of values has led to a unrest and indifference. All concerned appear to have lost their direction and sense of purpose resulting in demoralization among the teaching communities as well as the students. The beast in man is still pre-dominent. The evil traits like hatred, envy, greed, desire have to be uprooted. Only when this is achieved, our nation and the world can attain peace and joy. Education plays a crucial role at this juncture, it helps an individual cultivate the human values such as truth, righteousness or right conduct, peace, and non-violence.

There is a morality of reason, a morality proper to man and man's life is its standard of value. For existence on earth man's goals must choose it's actions and values for the purpose of preserving, fulfilling and enjoying the irreplaceable value, "his life". The revival of a society and the world depends upon a widespread renewal of individual commitment to an active value based life. ***The need of the hour is not to change the superstructure of educational system but its very foundation.***

"The focus today is describing and complaining about the things that are not working rather than on what works. We need to focus on what we are becoming not on what we are. Focus on what's left not what we lost or we are without."

—Gene Bedley.

National educator of the year America.

The beginning of the nineteenth century saw the rise of academics and polytechnics, that expanded the traditional concept of educational institutions and universities as the place for mainly humanistic studies, to cover provision for skills, to explore resource potential, to produce goods and services, to negotiate terms of transactions and to manage material wealth. The value system changed altogether and became the criteria used by the members of the society to evaluate objects., ideas, act, feeling or events as to their relative desirability, merits or correctness. Individual achievements or success through one's own effort started to be regarded as an important value as was the spirit of competition, with its corollary of the survival of the fittest. Hard work deferred gratification and continual striving were another set of highly valued ways to succeed. Individual freedom and material progress also became important values in life. The school system started giving emphasis on these aspects in their content, method and structure. Material progress became the indicator for development of a society. Emphasis on moral education reduced significantly in most countries of the world. Although principles of freedom, democracy, equality and justice remained as important values in spirit, educational agencies remained unconcerned about them in practice. People started laying emphasis on private property, the practice of capitalism, rationality and growth.

Today at the beginning of the twenty first century, the condition has no way improved. In fact today education has become increasingly secularized. There is too much emphasis on academic performance and equipping the student with technical skills. Education systems around the globe are designed to develop physical and intellectual aspects of human personality. Education is calculated to prepare students for employment and ignore the reality that students also need to prepare to meet the multifarious challenges of life. In today's education system, the emotional, the psychic and spiritual aspects of personality are ignored, with the result that students today receive inadequate and incomplete education. Thus despite intensive work the human personality remains underdeveloped.

As it appears, the schools and universities generally stopped making moral education an integral part of their curricula in the early part of this century because of the lack of cultural consensus and increase in religious and ethical differences.

Education System Focused for the New Millennium

Today what the world need is a rejuvenated educational system so as to save future generations from the clutches of progressive dilemma. 'Value centered classrooms' should be the slogan for the day, providing education which focuses on development of understanding, solidarity and tolerance among individuals and among ethnic, social, cultural and religious groups. Education can be the main instrument to promote knowledge, values, attitudes and skills conducive to respect human rights and to build a culture of peace and democracy. The education should enable one to utilise the knowledge one has acquired to meet the challenges of life. It must create a feeling in the minds of the students and should also cultivate a constant and continuous respect for human relationships.

The humanistic and valuistic dimensions of education should be investigated and education system should be cultivated on the belief that consensus on values is worth aiming for. Education imploring on the pillars of self-esteem both personal and cultural, respect and tolerance for different cultural groups, sense of belonging and responsibility towards one and all and an appreciation for the importance of learning hand in hand with ethical qualities required. In every individual a sense of universal values should be emphasized so that peace can prevail.

Education must emphasize on the development of ability to value freedom and the skills to meet it's challenges. It must develop the ability to recognize and accept the values, which exist in the diversity of individual, genders, people and culture, and develop the ability to communicate, share and co-operate with others. It must develop the ability of non-violent conflict resolution and promote the development of inner peace in the minds of students so that they can establish the qualities of compassion, tolerance, sharing and caring. It should also cultivate citizens to have the ability to make choices for their own selves, to give attention to environment and development of cultural heritage and sustain harmony between individuals, keeping in view connection between immediate basic needs and long term interests of the society. The education should also arm them to decide and formulate strategies to achieve their aims and aspirations within and the capacity of building a better world for their own self and for future generations to come.

This is the kind of value education we need the most at the dawn of the new millenium, in order for the young people to create their own identity. To develop a sense personal and social competence along with self-confidence, rational outlook and the ability to look at life as a whole. Complete control over one's self, is essential that will ultimately lead one to 'happiness', the successful state of life. Happiness is the state of consciousness, which proceeds from the achievement of one's values.

"A morality that dares to tell you to find happiness in the renunciation of your happiness, to value the failure of your values is an insolent negation of morality. By grace of reality and the nature of life man – every man is an end in himself, he exits for his own sake and the achievement of his own happiness is his highest moral purpose."

John Galt - "Atlas Shrugged"

Conclusion

Learning is essentially a process of internal transformation. A virtuous character is the end product of a process of unfolding of human perfection within. When this is achieved during moulding period of a child, it is reflected in the conduct of individual in the years to come. True education is a mixture of head and heart. We cannot be content with an education system, which is confined to academic achievement alone. Character development should be the foremost aim of education and central focus of all curriculum development exercises. It is only when the school or education system produces men and women of fine character will the world begin to see the fruits of large investments made in the 'production' of citizens. Thus the ultimate goal of value education is to include a greater range of human talent and a much more exclusive number of human beings, holding on to the dream that perhaps some day every body might be liberated by an education that stands in the service of human freedom.

REFERENCES

1. Bikas C. Synal. Need for Value-Based Education in the Twenty First Century, Paper submitted under topic "Education and Training for Peace" Internet.
2. M. N. Kalappa advocate, Mysore. Value-Based Education, Internet.
3. Dr. Deirdre, Mullan. Defining Value-Based Education, II European Meeting on Values Education, Northen Ireland, February 2001.
4. Shashank Shah, The Necessity of "Value-Based Education", Internet.
5. CYA TODAY September, 1999 Index of Articles, Value-Based Character Education: The Foundation of Correctional Education (December 1997) and Partnerships: A Quality Education for a Quality Life (April 1999).
6. Gordon Resnick, Value-Based Educator on a Mission Meredith.
7. National Educator of the Year Value-Based Educator on a Mission Education Must Be Value-Based and Free.

   Discourse given by Bhagwan on the 22-11-00 at Prashanti Nilyam during Convocation Day.
8. By Robert Merikangas, M.L.S., Ph.D. Values and Education in a Democracy: Resources for Conversations: An Annotated Heuristic Bibliography.

   Originally prepared in connection with the conference: "Teaching for Diversity, Unity, and Human Values: An Education Summit", University of Maryland

   College Park, MD, September 11-13, 1998.
9. Bell, Wendell. "Universal Human Values," pp. 171-227, in Values, Objectivity, and the Good Society, volume 2 of Foundations of Future Studies.

   New Brunswick, NJ: Transaction Publishers, 1997.

4

Value Learning & Curricular Dimensions at the Primary Level

P. Ananda
R.P. Pathak

A child learns values both informally and formally. However, value learning exclusively at home and neighbourhood will not fully suffice to develop all the desirable behaviours in the child to make him live in the society happily and peacefully. Therefore the school curriculum and the teachers have very important roles to play in the value development of the child. The National Curriculum Framework for School Education (NCERT 2000) has put considerable emphasis in formal learning on value education right from the formative years of schooling to the higher secondary stage (Class I to XII). The general objectives of education lay emphasis on a number of qualities that would make a child socially effective happy in future life.

Values represent our distinct behaviour pattern which may be treated by the society in different ways, e.g. acceptable or not acceptable, good or bad, cosmic or personal, and so on. The role of the parents, teachers, elders, schools and the community at large is to inculcate those behaviours in the child that would help establish a just society. After all, the kind of impression and qualities that the child develops during the primary school years have a direct bearing on his further schooling, career, and life. In this context, some of the important values intended to be culminated in the children at the primary level may be described as below:

Social Values: friendliness, cooperation, discipline, courage, love for work.

Moral Values: truthfulness, honesty, respect, courtesy.

Personal Values: punctuality, activeness, cleanliness, keeping healthy, neatness.

Spiritual Values: sacrifice, tolerance, forgiveness.

Emotional Values: love for one's country, extending help, voluntary service in need.

Aesthetic Values: love for beauty, love for nature, liking for anything good.

The categorization of values above are not based on any hard and fast logic and may be overlapping within categories.

Imparting value education is suggested not as a separate subject of study at any stage but has to be judiciously integrated with all subjects in the scholastic areas and other activities in non-scholastic areas. The value integration is emphasized in the general objectives of education stated in the national curriculum framework of which those having significance at the primary level could be stated as follows:

- development of scientific temper
- understanding of one's environment
- understanding of the diversity in lands and people
- appreciation of sacrifices and contributions made by eminent personalities
- knowledge of national symbols and their significance.
- developing deep sense of patriotism and nationalism.
- developing qualities related to personal, social, moral and spiritual values
- developing attitudes and habits for keeping fit physically and mentally
- appreciation for hard work and recognizing dignity of labour.

The educational objectives are to be achieved through certain media. In curricular terms, we call them as the **content** and the **learning experiences.**

Content:

By content we simply mean the subject matter in a field of study. This subject matter could be in the form of facts, concepts, ideas, skills, rules, principles, laws, theories etc. In other words, content may include all those things that man know and believe. Content is categorized into two types - Descriptive and Normative. Descriptive content is the one that contains factual knowledge which can be perceived directly or in principle. Books and such other literature are loaded with factual content. Normative content comprises rules, standards and norms by which people make moral and aesthetic choices. It contains the value standards men have built through generations. The objectives of education, the ideas operating in and through political institutions. The objectives of education, the ideas operating in and through political institutions, the legal systems, the rules of acceptable family conduct, etc. are examples of normative content.

The content deemed important to be imparted at the primary level are included under various subject titles in the national curriculum framework as given below:

A. Class I & II
   - One language - the mother tongue/regional language
   - Mathematics
   - Art of Healthy & Productive Living

B. Class III to V
   - One language - the mother tongue/regional language
   - Mathematics
   - Environmental Studies
   - Art of Healthy & Productive Living

Learning Experiences:

Learning experiences are mental operations that students employ in learning the content. In other words, it is the interaction between the learner and the external conditions in the environment to which he can react. Learning experiences give opportunities to the learners to practice the desired behaviour. They are the key factors that shape the learner's orientation to the content and ultimately the understanding of it. In practical terms, learning experiences include different **teaching methodologies** like lecture. Story telling, demonstration; **strategies** like multi-grade teaching, multi-level teaching; **curricular activities** like holding competitions of different nature, guest lecture on specific issues; and **co-curricular activities** like celebrating functions/events, organizing picnics/trips, etc. on different occasions.

The teacher has to take special interest and care in providing learning experience of different types to integrate values into the content. In this context, some of the specific methods that could be relevant at the primary level may include:

- story telling
- dramatization
- discussion
- role playing
- setting example by oneself (the teacher himself or herself)
- value clarification (while explaining content)
- exposing to incidents/places of value importance
- audio, video, film and multimedia exposure on relevant topics
- organizing curricular and co-curricular activities.

In actual learning both the content and learning experiences are in constant interaction. A teacher may adopt a special moral class for value teaching on few occasions but most of the time he/she is to integrate values through other teachings in such a manner that they are made acceptable to the learners. For specific curricular transaction with respect to value teaching at the primary level, Parida and Goswami (2001) have studied the curriculum of Environmental Studies (EVS) - Science for class III -V and have identified specific topic and corresponding value (s) associated with it which the teacher has to emphasize in teaching. An example derived from their study is cited below:

Subject : EVS - Science for Class III

Chapter: One (Things Around Us)

Topic: Things which are made by man/ not made by man

Value: We cannot repair or replace a natural thing. So we should not destroy nature (Kindness, concern for environment)

Value Learning and UEE Schemes:

The foregoing discussion and its implications are based on the assumption that the children are enrolled and studying in the schools. But what about those 6-14 years age group who are out of the formal school system? To address the problem of these groups, there have been various schemes under the banner of Universalisation of Elementary Education (UEE) since independence. The highly acclaimed scheme under implementation is the District Primary Education Programme (DPEP) which was launched as a centrally sponsored scheme in the year 1994. Starting with 42 districts in seven states in the beginning it has been expanded to 285 districts in 18 states now. Its primary focus is to bring out qualitative changes in primary education (Std. I - V at the moment) with stress on universal access, retention, improvement in learners achievement and reducing disparities among social groups. The broad objectives of the scheme explicitly speak of values like equality of educational opportunities while the qualitative changes in learning achievement do have value implications for learners implicitly. Since the DPEP scheme is going to be over by the year end or so, the Sarva Sikshya Abhiyan (SSA) is another scheme which is being further adopted by the states.

The DPEP scheme has a number of intervention areas to reach at its objectives, *viz.* community mobilization and participation; capacity building; pedagogical improvement; integrated education; innovations; planning, research and evaluation; supervision and monitoring, etc. On implementing the scheme, various DPEP states have adopted a number of programmes (events, innovations, projects, etc.) which have value implications not only for the children or learners but also for the community at large. A description of such programmes by some states as examples and their value significance is given below:

Program title & DPEP state	*Brief description*	*Inherent value*
School Readiness Centre (Assam)	To prepare children with special needs like physically handicapped, disadvantaged groups to join schools	kindness, fellow feeling, social justice
Raksha Bandhan Siksha Bandhan (Maharashtra)	On this day, Rakhis were tied to the out of school children (poor, those living in slums, streets) with a pledge to make them attend school	brotherhood, equality of opportunities
Camel Cart Library (Rajasthan)	A mobile library on the back of a camel to move from village to village to develop education awareness and learning	access to information reading habits
Mustiviksha (Orissa)	Children and teachers go door to door, collect alms from families and appeal people to send children to schools	generosity social responsibility

It may be observed that the above kinds of learning experiences which are primarily aimed at bringing children to the main stream of learning have also value implications. However, it is the teacher's interest and skills that would go a long way in integrating these values into the whole teaching - learning process.

REFERENCES

Diribsa D., Ananda P. et al (1999): Principles of Curriculum Inquiry (Distance Education Material). Addis Ababa University, Ethiopia.

Ministry of HRD (1998): DPEP Calling (Newsletter). Vol. III, December.

NCERT (2000): National Curriculum Framework for School Education, New Delhi, National Council of Educational Research & Training.

NCERT (1995): Special Orientation Programme for Primary Teachers (SOPT) New Delhi, National Council of Educational Research & Training.

Parida B.K., Goswami M. (2001): Strengthening Value Learning through EVSS. DPEP Calling (Newsletter). Vol. V, January - April.

5
Value Based Education in Society and Holistic Approach in Education Need of Hour

R.C. Nautiyal
Geetika Mehrotra

What is education? A parcel of books! Not at all but intercourse with world, with men and with affair. "We find that 'human values' play a very significant role in life of every student, and person of any caste and community."

It is fortunate to be a good person and in all situations goodness in strength. We should know the meaning of 'goodness. The first question, which comes to every one's mind is "What is the goal of human life?" The most realistic answer to this would be the attainment of happiness but he can equally be a cause of misery. A high position may be a cause of happiness but it can equally be a cause of misfortune.'

On the other side, it we follow truth, we are the first beneficiaries. But generally, the path of evil in more attractive in the beginning than the path of goodness. Due to this attraction one starts following the same. He also finds this path to be more crowded which removes his doubt. Once on the path of evil. He tends to remain there either due to ignorance or perhaps it is too late to change the course. While he discourages others too from following the path of goodness by giving them a false image of his happiness. There are four basic points, we may call them as fundamental values, which help in developing **Personality sensibility, honesty, responsibility** and **bravery.** For this we have to follow the four steps **self-inspection, self-fabrication, self-formation and self-development.**

The value that we need most to be fought to the human race is that life should be lived in pursuit of excellence even in the midst of difficult situation and struggle of daily life. Our troubles increase because we fail to differentiate between **Dharma** and **Adharma,** the Sreyas (the good) and the preyas (the pleasant). Our preferences for one or the other shapes our values that we hold in life. On set of values that fall in the **Sreyas** group leads human actions to the general good of mankind while the other that leads one to one pragmatic path of selfish pleasures falls in the **Preyas** group. Man as our worldly picture presents good for the **Preyas** and comes to grief in the end. Peace and happiness are hard to find. The prime task of education, therefore, should be to enable man to modify and recognise his value system in the desired way of the **sreyas** the good and make continual progress towards a better world.

The educated classes of country slid from ecstasy of freedom to rank selfishness and human unconcern after the nations's independence. Although our constitution contains all provisions with good ideas for all-round developments in every area, so that every citizen may make himself happy but it somehow failed to stress the fundamental duties of citizen, because stress have only been given on fundamental right continuously till date. Consequently, the dignity of the individuals and unity of nation have taken the back seat. As such we have failed to inspire a sense of responsibility in every walk of life.

Why did we remain undeveloped nation even after more than 50 years of political freedom. The answer is that we failed to develop the means of national development, *i.e.*, (*i*) education on national scale. (*ii*) self-discipline, hard and co-operative work culture, and (*iv*) humanistic impulse. Majority of the people in our society are content at seeing nothing beyond their little horizones of a few yards, *i.e.* the routine work: eating, drinking, learning and begetting following each other in mathematical precision. Almost all such people became obsessed with wealth only. While plutocrats of United State of America as Bill Gate of Microsoft and Jim Stowers the Kansas Financier to Holly Wood, etc. are now taking steps to ensure their children do not fall victim to "affluenza" the moral, emotional and practical programs associated with having money- by donating their huge sum to charity organization.

A nation can't become great without self-discipline and the self-discipline in the mark of a freeman while indiscipline is the mark of a slave. The fact that we are still a highly indisciplined people and also raided with petty jealousies which only shows that we have not shed our slave mentality. Though external political freedom has come to us, unfree India have had more free people than free individuals and as a result of not using the freedom to transform Indian society, we could not become a highly developed one because our people used their intelligence only to advance one-self and in total naglect of the nation. We, therefore have to make our people as **"human"** instead a candidate of humanity.

The Bhagwata Gita's philosophy of education linked with values—**Kama, Artha, Dharma** and **Moksha** are more in practice by people outside India than the people within India. '**Kama**', desire which constitutes the entire range of human determination at the sensory level. Artha, Wealth is the instrument for the satisfaction fo Kama. 'Dharma' or ethical sense helps discipline and regulate the persuit of **Kama** and **Artha.** When man as a person or as an enlightened citizen becomes person of human values, he does not think of himself but he thinks that he has been called upon by the nation to perform services to the people. This service to the society has been taught in the Bhagwaga Gita to derive the true joy in life. *i.e.* **Moksha,** which may be experienced as a product of man's inner growth (spiritual growth) free from individuality. This comprehensive philosophy of life and action in the system of education techniques are required to be introduced in order to achieve the objectives of total human orientation.

What we need to do at this juncture, it is to leave aside the western philosophy and methods in field of Indian education system and have to create now a conducive climate where novel ideas are encouraged and valued to result in a better development. In order to achieve this object we are required to identify and introduce the missing link of our religion and interpersonal situations in the system of education as had been in practice in our age old system. Gurukul system of education, which were full of values and virtues based on the knowledge of our own philosophy of life and culture.

REFERENCES

1. Sharma, S.L. (1994), Role of Education in India's Development. Academician (March), 4 (1), 17-20.
2. Speech: on Value Education : Prof. Pramod Bhatnagar Shantikunj, Haridwar.
3. Sinha. S.N.P Towards Inculcating Values in Education, University News 39 ()43.
4. Bossard, J.H.S. (1948) The Sociology of Child Development. New York: Harper.

6
Value Based Education: A Wide Spectrum

Purnima Srivastava

Vallabh Bhai Patel, the great architect of modern India once observed "Education without value is of no use". Education is a powerful and pervasive agent for all round development, individual and social transformation . This alone can sustain culture and civilization. The time has come to introspect the very meaning of quality education, weather in schools or in colleges or in universities. Through the passage of time, we have seen from Gurukul education to cyberspace education, how these values have changed. The rate at which the changes are happening is very fast and is pushing the traditional values aside. This transition may be the result of modernization and globalization of our education, which affected the life style of human being. There is chaos and confusion every where and at every step of educational system and machinery. Thus, it needs a drastic reconstruction almost a revolution.

The greatest challenges the world is facing today, are the crises of confidence and character, mental and moral decay and breakdown of traditional discipline. The root causes of all these are fear, hatred and greed. Therefore, it is in the mind of such person that the struggle must be waged to eliminate these divisive forces. This is possible only by true education - which involves harmonious development of body, mind and spirit.

Ravindra Nath Tagore had a vision for such an education, "Education must aim at the development of moral, spiritual and ethical values and we should seek them in our own heritage as well as in other cultures and civilizations. It should be such that Indians do not lose sight of their rich heritage - their thought must be noted to the ideals set forth in the great writings and works of our sages, poets and philosophers".

The university education commission,, Secondary education commission, Kolhari commission and Rama Murti Commission reports have all advocated and recommended spiritual training and introduction of ethical and moral instruction. They have also emphasized its role in the growth and building of characters. They went in great depth to recommend conscious efforts for the development of social, moral and spiritual values with the help of ethical teachings of the great religious teachers.

Education in Human Values

The word education in the ordinary sense of the term means literacy, formal education, getting through examinations and acquisition of knowledge. Knowledge does not mean bookish knowledge but one studied with noble feelings and values of life such as power and virtue. The concept and process of education facilitates the physical, mental, social, emotional and spiritual development of a person. Education is a process in which we lead from the innate knowledge. An education is a process in which occurs the manifestation of perfection and divine already present in man. So a quality education is a service to society and ultimately to the nation.

The objective of education should not be learning or teaching of social, Physical, Biological or Medical sciences, but the growth of body, mind and soul. It should be aimed at happiness, compassion, friendliness and adoption of human values. Thus every university should work at value-oriented education and idealistic socio spiritual patterns. If it is there, a nation will be able to prosper and the people of the nation will grow in stature, which was the dream of our beloved poet Ravindra Nath Tagore. Only then the lives of the poor people of India will be happier, richer and fuller which was the dream of Pt. Jawahar Lal Nehru. Only then every tear from every eye will be wiped away which was the dream of the father of our nation, Mahatma Gandhi. Only then India will be able to occupy the foremost place amongst all the progressive nations of the world.

The Kothari Commission report reiterates that education should become an instrument of social, economical and political change and thereby directed towards the realisation of the people's aspirations for national development. Therefore, at this crucial juncture when we are in 21st century, university should also concentrate:

1. To ensure social equality and justice.
2. To develop the qualities of good character and strong leadership.
3. To inculcate an ability for life long learning and develop a sense of dignity.
4. To eradicate illiteracy and ensure uniform education.
5. To give equal importance to scholarship and humanism.
6. To develop nationalistic feelings among the students. There is a need for strong patriotism again with the spirit of commitment. Educational institutions will have to create a healthy atmosphere of national unity, integrity and communal harmony.
7. To induce positive attitude in the students, for this teacher will have to know what teaching is all about. The meaning of teaching is not only the covering of the syllabus, but the uncovering of the syllabus to the students so that the students may feel the subject, smell the flavour of it, experience the beauty of the subject and got excited to learn it. Thus teaching can be made more meaningful by giving the importance of the noble values of life such as concentration, truthfulness, honesty, wisdom and love.

In such a manner human values can take proper place in our educational system, then only there is a hope of regeneration of India. So let us first build our character and then rebuild our great nation.

Values and Holistic Approach in Education

The development of values is not a very easy job. There is no magic formula, technique or strategy for the inculcation and development of values. The process of value education is a very complicated task, influenced by a variety of hereditary and environmental factors. Generally, value education programme involves direct, indirect and incidental approaches of value development. Direct approach refers to deliberate systematic instruction in specially provided periods in the school timetable. Through indirect approach value education is imparted through regular subjects of school curriculum and co-curricular activities. Whenever the value inculcation and development are resorted to, in relation to a specific event or situation that actually occurs in the school, is known as incidental approach of value education.

These days a new approach called holistic approach comes in existence. From holistic viewpoint different identities are based on the nature of wholes within wholes. If one identity is a part in relation to a larger whole it is also simultaneously a whole in relation to other identities deemed as its integral parts. This holistic concept of whole within whole transcends the traditional whole part dualism which, for instance is related in the differentiation of national and regional languages, or in the majoritarian culture and the minoritatian subcultures.

Value-Based Teachers

If contemporary education is to be value based, it can never be done without the teachers themselves understanding, appreciating and upholding the life sustaining moral values. The teachers cannot have any excuse what so over. If one cannot practice these values, one should not dream of teaching as a job. In fact, teaching is not a job, it is a mission and vision for life and for posterity. ***Swami Vivekanand*** established Ramakrishana Mission Order in 1897. Now there are a number of educational institutions administered by Ramakrishana Mission throughout the country. They are transmitting the universal values of austerity, brotherhood, compassion, dedication, empathy, faithfulness, grace, hard work, integrity, justice, kindness, liberty, mercy, nonviolence, obedience, rationality, selflessness, truth, unity, virtue, wisdom and yoga.

Eternal and universal values makes human life meaningful

on the earth. Today life appears to be meaningless and monotonous, because the people are not adequately sensitive to practicing the timeless moral values. Teachers being the custodians and communicators of values need to become value based. Then there can be value-based education. Teachers have to play a vital role. Thus the former president ***Dr. Shankar Dayal Sharma*** had said, "Thus a teacher must succeed in conveying the larger ideals of service to the community, virtues of tolerance and respect for all faiths, the importance of character, integrity and discipline and the value of humanism to his pupils. They should also be aware of our heritage and culture".

Science and Spirituality in the Core of Education

The Indian culture is deeply rooted in spiritual values and unless the values find their way into the life of students, education will lose its significance and will not fulfil its function of endowing the students with a vision to live by and with the ideals to work for. Therefore, in difference to the cherished goals of democracy, socialism, humanism and secularism, it is very essential that our educational system should evolve a new positive morality, which could effectively be built into school curriculum.

Any institution run by government or non-government organisation should create a secular atmosphere in the premises and the students should be taught the responsibilities of good citizens. There should not be any implication on caste, race and sex in any curriculum. Traditional courses should not only be updated by incorporating new methodologies and theories, at the same time it should be supported with ample number of examples which are relevant to the courses. The innovations in science and technology, the personal contributions, etc. should be explored and studied from the application point of view. Information exchange should not only be an import or export of knowledge but also be of inspirational nature.

It is essential that the teachers also should be exposed to the traditional values and others of education through training programme from time to time. They should confine themselves to their jobs to a more formality of completing the syllabus and following the curriculum. There should be a platform for teachers to deliberate on any sensitive issues or topics as and when the need arises. They should also explore the ideas of accepting modernization, globalization and liberalization from the academic point of view. They should also learn while imparting their duties for which they are meant. By creating a conducive atmosphere for intellectual rigor and freedom of expression and thought one can put value in education. The glory of education is the discovery of the soul. From primary to university stage, educational system should impart spiritual techniques and encourage sports and cultural activities. NCC and NSS, yogic meditation has stood the test of science, psychiatry and medical experiments. We must also put emphasis on the study of the life of great sons of the earth whose ideas and ideals have moved the world. It will provide an insight for character development and spiritual direction.

The primary task of education is the creative extension of knowledge, but it is not the total task. The educator's task is a holistic task, and one cannot say to the students that he will take care only of their minds. Young people at their school and university should be given an understanding of moral and spiritual·values. If education has a relationship with the meaning of life, then a proper value orientation of education becomes imperative.

If we want education to become a powerful and pervasive agent for revolutionary social transformation and a key that unlock the door of all round progress of the nation - let the educational system adopt these ideals.

REFERENCES

Hariharan, R., "Values & Ethics in Technical Education", "University News", Vol. 41, No. 32, June, 2003.

Murlidharan, K., "Values in Education: A changing Perspective", "University News," Vol. 40, No. 1, Jan., 2002.

Mohanty, A., "Integration of Human Values in Teacher Education," University News, Vol. 41, No. 34, August, 2003.

7

Students Deviant Behaviour and Education of Values

B.P. Uniyal

The thinking about values had always been a perpetual phenomenon in societies. Since the evolution of human race, its existence is discussed with concept and action in perspective of change in time. The societies having tribal basis still upheld their values intact without having any significant transformation. They disseminate these values by their deeds and living with them to one to another generation by informal way of education. But the societies of so-call advanceness owe the gratitude of advancing values up to the level of exaltation has now been witnessing the worse degeneration of values in all forms.

Our colleges and campuses are even not remain untouched by this deterioration. Today's youth are faced up several hang up and are suffering from prejudiced of class and caste divisions, corrupt influence of money and open defiance of norms of justice and equality causing in results of social and academic chaos. The people all over the world have now started to think that education of science, technology and other physical progress itself does not seem to be enough. There is definitely something beyond these all to provide peace, tranquillity, fraternity and universal brotherhood among the people. For this we need to re-explore, exercise and expand the age old generational spiritual values, a perfect blend of Karma, artha, dharma and moksha effectively.

The paper is an effort to explain those psycho-social and educational factors which seems to be responsible to generate disruptive behaviours among the students and whose root exists with the devaluation of values. The inculcation of values and value education, which are guiding stars for students may provide motivational force for thought, emotion and action to bring about peace, progress and welfare in the campuses both individually and collectively.

Deviation Behaviour

Briefly to explain, students hyperactivity and deviate behaviour usually is referred to students' participation in those activities which are generally assumed to be anti-social and anti-academic, which has sometime political and social implications, organised demonstrations, strikes, rallies, walk-outs, assaults and destroying private and public property and paralell likewise activities in and out of campus - all are considered as constituents of deviant behaviour. Various psycho-social, educational and socio-economic correlates are inter-linked with problem which are obviously genesized due to degenerations of values, i.e. ethical and human.

The ***overcrowededness of schools and colleges*** has lost the personal touch and discredited the sacred ties of the teacher and discipline as of yore. The heavy syllabus has made short work of moral education. The ***lack of teacher-student relationship*** has aggravated the impersonalness among the students. The bond of respect of individual personality, impression, feelings and affection seems to be difficult to establish healthy relationship. It has now been seen more political rather than academic and spiritual. Humyun Kabir (1977) rightly observed the general ***loss in indealism*** as one of the reason of disrupt behaviour. The spread of materialistic ideology undermined the sense of values by its insistence that ends justified the means.

In no other country, the university system is so closely involved in politics as in India. Every party has got their student wings which not only seeks the moral support but also monetary assistance. This ***political contamination*** has violated the climate and demoralised the dedicated enhancement. ***Lack of harmonious culture,*** rising frustration, generational conflict, weak teacher personal devotional lack, unethical practices and various others are observed as responsible for disruptive behaviour. Some time very insignificant correlates were been observed as subjected to disruption of behaviour among the students. Many personality hypertraits, i.e. aggression, intolerance, irritability, unstable, violent, moody, etc. seems an outburst of the results of these factors.

Possible Solution - Value Education

The value education most become an integral part of the entire education by weaving the values into programmes. It should be started with the early stages of education in order to have a lasting effect on the prospect of conduct and the way of life. There is a popular saying that morality is caught not taught. Therefore, the only way to influence the values of children in school or college is through the organization and atmosphere of the school including the personal examples set by the teachers. The value education if properly brought in practice it could definitely be able to lead a society of personality, brightness and behavioural normalcy. By doing the following activities which are an expression of value orientation, we may normalise and passify the disruptive behaviours upto certain extent and induce them the motivation of eternalise of values.

- The inculcation of superrational value of Truth (Satya) may provide them a common super-ordinate identity based on divinity. The appreciation of shared common identity by man serves to eliminate socially division basis. Thus caste, creed, religion sect, ideology become irrelevant. The whole mankind is seen as belonging to a single caste humanity.
- The internal calmness protects the mental and physical health of individual. An internal serene person can withstand situation of great psychological stress. He can remain undamaged by tension, turmoil and unrest.
- The famous Sanskrit saying Udar-charitnam tu Vasudhaiva Kutumbakani may well be able to disseminate to the

feeling of universal brotherhood and fraternity.

- The inculcation of love and affection eliminate the motivation for revenge, crime, cruelty, exploitation, violence. It also helps in repair and restoration of broken interpersonal relationship.
- Work on community basis should be included as a part of inculcation of values. It may foster many valuable traits among the students.
- A student should be encouraged to think of wrong impulses not as a sin or offence but as curable diseases so that he may start to think that improvement can be done at any time.
- The teacher needed to exercise justifiable decisions frankly without any partiality to any part.
- Dhyana, Sadhna, Shravana and Manan can confer the strength, needed to meet the challenges of life effectively.
- The teacher should bring his student nearer to the realization of the ideals. Children have their own daily battles of loyalties and friendship and there are moments of desperate depression and violent enthusiasm. The teacher on these occasions can show the truth and the awakening of right sense and the right direction of the progress. The inculcation of values like tolerance, cooperation, mutual respect, goodness, Ahimsa, faith, forgiveness, simplicity and honesty shall definitely be able to help modify, restructure, and control deviation and disruption of behaviour into a desired and integrated personal development.

REFERENCES

Allport, G.W., Values in Our Youth, Teacher College Record, 1961.

Joshi Kireet, An outline – Pedagogical Suggestions, In S.P. Ruhela (Ed.) Human Values and Education, Sterling Publications, New Delhi, 1986.

Rastogi, P.N., Reconstruction of Social System, In S.P. Ruhela (Ed.) Human Values and Education, Sterling Publications, New Delhi, 1986.

Uniyal, B.P. Student Activism and Interest Paradigm of Students, University News, AIU, New Delhi, 1993.

8
Education in Human Values

S.K. Joshi
C.S. Shukla

"Education has an accelerating role, it refines sensitivities and perceptions that contribute to national cohesion, a scientific temper and independence of mind and spirit thus furnishing the goals of socialism, secularism & democracy enshrined in our constitution".

—National policy on education, 1986.

Education with the aim of all round development of personality, started in the sacred heart of Gurukuls. As the time passed off and reached to the present scenario, education has seen a tremendous changes due to the need & demand of the society. In the juvenile steps of twenty first century, the world is facing a bunch of problems which includes terrorism, population explosion, pollution, etc. Our beloved country India, the birth place of many religions & the world's largest democratic country, is also facing the cancerous attack of communalism, terrorism and other social and political problems. Intellectuals searched and researched the problems. Each problem has several reasons but the core reason for each one is "Value Crisis". Universally it is accepted that education and society are interdependent. So, it can be assumed that for every malfunctioning of society, education is responsible and to get out of that, education system has to be worked upon.

From the time immemorial, alongwith the development of cognitive skills, teaching of values has been a crucial educational aim. Whereas now we are contented only with the development of knowledgeable & skilled individuals. It was recognized for a longtime that there is a need for adding a fourth R to stand for RESPONSIBILITY to the traditional 3 Rs. *i.e.* reading, writing & arithmetic. Every society cherishes the ideal of having good citizens. By good citizens we mean responsible, participative members of the society. The society through education carries out enculturation, of the young, to shoulder the obligations and the responsibilities of the society. It is through education that the culture of the society can be preserved or conserved. The most essential part of a culture undeniably is its value system. Education has, therefore, a very important functions of inculcating the desirable values in the pupil.

Education in human values refers to a wide range of learning and activities which includes training in physical health, mental hygiene, etiquette and manners, appropriate social behaviour, civil rights and duties to aesthetic and even religious training. Whenever, education in any field has to be thought about the objectives of such education must be clear in the mind. Objectives, whether of value education or of any other curricular area, depend on a variety of factors—psychological, sociological & epistemological. The ancient Hindus recommended the pursuit of three important impersonal values : Truth (Satyam), Goodness (Shivam) and Beauty (Sundaram) & four personal values of Dharma (Religiousness), Artha (Wealth), Kama (Desire) and Moksha (Self-Realization). Now the time has changed, modern society is more complex & there are varieties of social demands made on the people. A civilized individual must possess certain minimum social skills such as he/she may have to transact business in his private or public capacity, he/she has to function as a citizen of his/her state, of his/her country and of the world and much more. So in order to educate the individual regarding the human values, the report of the Joint Study on Moral Education in Asian countries (JSMEA) lists the following objectives for value education.

1. Full development of child's personality in its physical,

mental, emotional and spiritual aspects.

2. Inculcation of good manners and responsible and cooperative citizenship.
3. Developing respect for the dignity of the individual and the society.
4. Inculcation of a spirit of patriotism and national integration.
5. Developing a democratic way of thinking and living.
6. Developing tolerance towards and understanding of different religious faiths.
7. Developing a sense of human brotherhood at the social, national and international levels.
8. Helping children to have faith in some supernatural power and order that is supposed to control this universe & human life.
9. Enabling children to make moral decisions on the basis of sound moral principles.

These objectives must cover the cognitive, conative and affective domains so that the learner could be educated in the real sense, i.e. he/she is able to think right, to feel the right kind of emotions and to act in the desirable manners.

Can values be taught in a formal way? Not entirely. They have to be 'caught' in environment. They are to be lived, like a science course. They have to be practiced in the home/society laboratory. However, the content of the value education must include—

(*a*) Social & ethical values, examples from day-to-day situations, extracts from sayings of great men, incidents and problems which develop value judgement among pupils, dramas, dialogues, simple poems and scriptures from world religions could form the major part of the content alongwith the biographies of great men.

(*b*) Personal, neighbourly and community values should be taught in the classroom and thoroughly discussed with the students.

(*c*) A variety of learning resources can be used for value education ranging from biographies, scriptures, proverbs, hymns and sayings of great men to current social and political events, stories from religion and mythology, moral dilemmas and school events.

(*d*) Yoga and other activities that develop self-discipline among students could be included.

(*e*) Group activities like cleaning the school campus, visiting slums, service campus, visits to hospitals, visit to places of worship of different faiths should form part of content in value education.

(*f*) Personality development retreats could be held to enable the students to develop self control, punctuality, sharing and caring, respect for other faiths, co-operation and the value of silence (inner peace).

(*g*) Prayer meditation and shramadan could form part of the content of value education. They can help the students cultivate inner poise and an attitudinal shift, and develop the quality of dignity of labour.

(*h*) Observing jayantis, i.e. birthdays of great national and spiritual leaders and organizing youth organizations for character development like "Balaka Sangha" or Taruna Sangha can go a long way in the cultivation of values in students.

Education is a process of bringing about desirable changes of behaviour in the individual in his/her knowledge, skills, attitudes and values. The school seeks to achieve this through its curriculum, which is nothing but the sum total of all its organized activities. Curriculum thus, essentially has a value basis. Apart from the values that are imparted through what is called as the 'hidden curriculum' of the school, value education is also provided explicitly and deliberately as a subject in the school curriculum. Our concern here is with the strategies and methods of such value education. At the outset, we should recall that value education is a complex process which involves developing the ability to think morally, the ability to do 'right' thing and also the ability to feel the right emotions. Naturally, therefore, there can be no single method for value education. In value education literature, three methods of imparting value education are usually mentioned. The direct method, the indirect method & the incidental method. The direct method of value education refers to deliberate, systematic attempt by the teacher to teach values as a subject or an area of thought, This method aims at acquainting the pupils consciously and overtly with the skills, techniques and qualities required to get the right answers to moral questions and giving them practice involving moral problems. Such a method might include regular class room instruction, talk and discussion to develop knowledge and understanding of values, discussions of situations involving value conflicts, presenting students with value dilemmas and developing the ability to make sound value judgement. In the indirect method, value education is given indirectly as a by-product of teaching a particular subject. It is assumed that all educational effort is aimed at value development, for eg. while teaching language the overt objective will be to develop language ability. But the remote objective is to enable a person to communicate with other and also the content included under language can be so arranged and exploited as to yield objectives of value education. The third method is the incidental method. Many incidents which can be labelled as right or wrong do ordinarily occur in every school. Their frequency may be high or low depending upon several factors. The advocates of this method see in such incidents opportunities for value education and want them to be exploited for the purpose. The right actions have to be go with a reward, a word of praise of encouragement. Where as misdeeds, petty or serious, have to be negatively reinforced or punished, because many children will not be really aware of what is right or wrong.

For providing education in human values, any method or group of methods can be adopted. Since values are not such a thing which could be imposed on anyone, therefore, the following are suggested to promote growth of values:

(*a*) Encourage pupils to make choices on their own and to make them choose freely without any fear or hesitation.

(*b*) Help pupils discover and examine the alternatives that are available for choosing.
(*c*) Help the pupils to weigh the consequences of each alternative and the actions that ensure.
(*d*) Encourage pupils to think and understand what they prize and cherish and therefore value.
(*e*) Provide the pupils opportunities to demonstrate their choices & discuss the consequences.
(*f*) Encourage the pupils to act in accordance with their choices.

Teachers role cannot be separated as a value education for value education is inbuilt in the business of teaching itself. There are three prominent areas in which the teacher can influence the value development of his children. First, in the subject he/she teaches, he/she must be aware of the values and moral demands, lying hidden in the curriculum that can be developed at the time of teaching. The depends upon the teachers' skill & proficiency of doing so, secondly the teacher should establish and maintain clear standards of behaviour and encourage his/her pupils to behave towards himself/herself, towards one another and towards the whole community in an orderly and considerable way. Lastly, the teacher has to help pupils become free and rational adults by personal example. It is well-known fact that example exerts a more powerful influence than precept. He/she should provide for the children a model of a free and rational adult in his/her interpersonal relations through his/her conduct & reactions to the day-to-day incidents of school life.

Schools, also have an important role in value education. Value development will be taking place constantly both within and outside the school, influenced by a complex network of environment factors—home, peer group, media & the community at large. The extent to which school functions effectively as training grounds for values depends on their physical condition, and the professional idealism of teachers among other things. To the extent, the school factor such as teacher with? teacher, teacher with pupil, teacher with parent and the various other group interaction the school traditions

& values, the curricular and co-curricular activities the school & climate influence the value development of children, schools have a responsibility in exercising over these and creating conducive conditions for the value development of children.

Human values have a vast circumference, so it is difficult to have an approach to all points. But education is also a life long process and to reach to the ideal position is always the ultimate aim of education. Infact education in human values is an unending process and its nature is ever changing. With the change in society, political system, economical system or cultural system. The objectives curriculum & methods of value education continuously changes, therefore, the education in human values require continuous search & research as per the need of the society.

REFERENCES

1. Chilana M.R. & Dewan M.L; The human values, A task for all, 1998 Edn., Concept Publishing Company, New Delhi, P.P-203-207.
2. Dewey, John; Moral principles in education, New York, Philosophical Library, 1959.
3. Gupta. N.L., Neo-Humanism & human values, 1999 Edu., Mohit publication, New Delhi- P.P 165-169.
4. Rimse, Mysore: Report of the proceedings of the National Seminar on Value education, Ramakrishna Institute of Moral and Spiritual Education, 1986.
5. Shukla J.D., Report of the Moral Education Committee, U.P. 1983.

9
Education in Human Values

Kusum Lata Rathor

Man is an endless aspiring medium of consciousness. The meaning of man is so comprehensive that it includes in its scope all the qualities of man both intrinsic and extrinsic. The intrinsic attributes of man which constitute his 'essence' indicate his richness and greatness. Our ultimate concern, whatsoever it may be, give focus and unit to our personality, and when the content of this concern is truly ultimate, then a faith in spiritual powers, in the proper sense of the term arises. The experience of numinous, the divine experienced as wholly other, majestic and powerful are the content of such a faith. Man is supreme of all the creations of this universe due to rare qualities which are not found in any other species of the world. He is a master of higher reason called 'intuition' that makes him the king of all creation.

On the other hand is a social being and it is the man who can realize that social good and social reform must have some end beyond the promotion of mere physical comfort and material satisfaction. The moment he transcends these limitations of social reform and physical comfort and searches for a higher satisfaction, he becomes an ideal.

Values govern the moral universe of man. But more important of all is that they operate through his unconscious self to awaken his inherent aspiration to become more and more subtle and spiritual. Hence, values may be described as a system of personality traits, which are in harmony with the inner nature of an individual and which are in accordance with the values approved by the society. The process of valuing is what we go through when we make judgement about things, events and people that we encounter in our day to day life. To understand life in its total dimension means contrition because every moral achievement stands under the criticism of a more essential goodness. If is not only wanting in perfect goodness, but there is something of the perversity of evil in it. Such contrition does not destroy selfishness in the human heart. But there is a difference between the man who understands somethings of the mystery of evil in his own soul and one who complacently accepts human egoism as a force which must be skilfully balanced with altruism in order that moral unity may be achieved.

At present, the conception of value has enlarged so much that every thing good and useful has been included in its scope. For example the qualities like-honestly, devotion self-respect, courage, sacrifice, etc. which were long branded as virtues and attributes, are classed under the general classification of values. All branches of knowledge impart values in their own way. The new claims, the new standards, the new ambitions of the modern world are also values, today. For lower conscious medium of life, every fact is value in itself. As they grow and evolve, they are bound to shed off these normal levels of evaluation. Higher and higher norms are beginning to operate and this process will be continuous one. So the value-ideals evolve with the emerging awareness or consciousness of the individual.

The proverb "when wealth is lost nothing is lost, when health is lost something is lost, when character is lost everything is lost", was a motivating peculiar way in which a wiseman of the older generation defined philosophically the importance of character in human life. It may be said that life without character has no clear destiny and value, for it is the character of the mind that decides the destiny, value, dignity and status of man and makes him a rational being in the true sense of the word. Character is the pillar of strength in human life without that the mind will be crippled and behaviour disfigured. In a nutshell, it can be said that it is the spiritual and moral element in the mind that shapes and sharpens the mental faculty of man.

Values keep on changing at every age with experience, but at no time in life, an average man or woman is likely to be concerned about values and standards as much as during adolescant period. It is a transitional period when ideas and values consolidate. Youth, who are physically well-built, healthy, energetic and efficient; mentally well developed, thoughtful, knowledgeable and innovative; psychologically enthusiastic and zestful, can lead a nation to the golden age. If the youth of a country are of high character and creative, then all the people will have a sound character and constructive habits. Hence, we should teach values to our children because it is the most significant and effective thing we can do for their happiness as educationists and parents.

Value Types:

Real knowledge is all-inclusive and integral. So, the values are now considered as total modes of human behaviour including-physical, vital, mental, psychical and spiritual. In academic philosophy values are popularly interpreted as extrinsic and intrinsic.

Extrinsic values:

Under the category of extrinsic value, we may include physical or economic values. These values are, however, instrumental and changeable. In almost all philosophies of the world, physical objects form the framework for all evolution and growth. The whole society and its working is grounded on economic values. In my opinion, in an economy of democratic society, on the part of decision-makers, some values like personal efficiency, public spirit pervasive human concern and resistance to social injustice are required for human excellence.

Intrinsic Values:

Intrinsic values are ends in themselves and are not convertible or exchangeable. They are things-in-themselves. Absolute values like, truth, goodness, beauty, love and friendship, etc. are categorised as values of intrinsic nature.

These values influence the authentic individuality of a person in many ways, "Truth" is a logical ideal, the absolute reality and the teat of an event. Human progress is conditioned by this ideal*. Soren Kierkegaard, an eminent existentialist, says that 'truth' lies in subjectivity rather than in objectivity because the objective accent falls on 'what' is said, the subjective accent on "How" it is said, Objectively the interest is focused merely on the thought-content, subjectively on the inwardness. At its maximum this inward "how" is the passion of the infinite' and the passion of the infinite is the truth. But the passion of the infinite is precisely subjectivity and thus subjectivity becomes the truth. Objectively there is no infinite decisiveness and hence, it is objectively in order to annul the difference between good and evil; together with the principle of contradiction and therewith also the infinite difference between the true and the false. Only in subjectivity there is decisiveness, to seek objectivity is to be in error. It is the passion of the infinite that is the decisive factor and not its content, for its content is precisely itself. In this manner subjectivity and the subjective 'how' constitute the truth.

'Goodness' is the intrinsic reality, the standard norm, the absolute entity or perfection. Norms like "greatest good for all" explain the social ideal in their own way. Humanist classified social relationship is the categories, I-You and I-It. The I-You relationship in one of intimacy, mutuality, sharing and trust. The I-It relationship is one of having, using, exploiting. To pul it in different terms, the I-It relationship is one- way form of relating in which the I give to and receives from you. Example of these two types of relationship are easy to find in our society. Anyone who has ever dealt with a large bureaucracy, the huge organization, or perhaps even registered for college courses, knows what it ıs like to be treated as a thing. When one is treated as an "it", there is no mutually; the one so treating you has only an interest in getting something from you and is totally unconcerned about relating to you as a person. When we relate to another person as a you, we do not treat that person as a thing of an object.

There is nothing wrong with the I-it relationship per se as

long as it is limited to things, to objects. But to treat a person as a thing, as an it, is to debase not only the other person but to sacrifice one's own humanity as well . We become human only through genuinely human relationship, I-You relationship, and when we treat a you as an it, we loss something of our own humanness. Martin Buber, an eminent humanist, suggests that it is possible to sustain I-You relationship with animals, trees, flowers and even inanimate objects. A logger surveying a stand of timber and calculating the number of board feel that will result when the trees are harvested has only an I-It relationship with the forest. The logger is concerned only with exploiting the resources of the forest and marketing the lumber successfully to make the largest possible profit. This is not the only way to relate to a tree or to a forest. Basking in the shades of a tree, contemplating it, writing a poem about it, marvelling at its wonder and complexity-all these signal an I-You relationship. An I-you relationship with a family pet whose whole life is focused on the relationship. An I-You relationship with a family pet whose life is focused on the relationship with the family is experienced by all of us.

"Beauty" may be subjective, objective or integral. Thus the classification of beauty and its gradation is directly related to its evaluation methods and processes. Eminent philosophers of 20th century proclaim that freedom, love, brotherhood and truth are the highest values to be gained. For Nietzsche the highest value is 'love', that is whole and holy. Through Zarathustra (Superman of his imagination) he preaches a gospel which is more liberal and more psychologically enlightened than Christianity. Jaspers advises for treating one's neighbour as oneself. He finds the necessity of communication between people for the realization of inner existence. According to Marcel, love, freedom and truth are interrelated and they cannot be separated from each other, but they can be looked as values by a man who has placed himself within the axis of intelligible light. In fact, love is the native capacity of man. In the domain of religion, this love is transformed into as act of self-surrender. We can say that all sense of sacrifice, duty and attachment to the family, neighbourhood, nation and humanity, is but, the outcome of love in man.

Psychic values which are intrinsic in nature, are higher values. These are rooted in volitional and material nature of the individual, in-thinking, feeling and willing. For the ability to accept, evaluate and adopt new ideas, value-consciousness is required in a man. In the development of value-consciousness some faculties like- 'sensitiveness', 'reason', 'free-will' and 'aspiration' which engender and sustain 'hope', play a major role.

The foundation of India's growth, strength, religion and culture are the basic values of "Satyam, Shivam and Sundaram", and they have their source from soul . These are embodiment of intellectual, ethical and aesthetic values and constitute the 'essence' of spiritual reality. In a vide sense, all the individual and social values are included in them. In 'Satyam', values like honesty, justice, freedom, courage, purity, etc.; in 'Sundaram, values like excellence, joy, love, cleanliness, respectability and etiquette, etc. are included.

This is an age of crises. We find lack of moral and spiritual values all around the world. Science and technology that has given enormous power to people, are incapable of coping with consequences because other aspects of personality have not grown commensurately with material development. It is tragic that in the very country, India, which gave birth to these spiritual ideas to the world, there is vast erosion of all values. Today, various communicating agencies are growing rapidly like TV Internet in computers and news papers, etc. and they are influencing our society in a great manner. Students are living with these means so many hours a day. The programmes and material provided by these agencies playing a major role in making the personality of the children. That is one of the major cause for the erosion of values because these are motivated by material gains and paying no head on the values of our country. Nietzsche finds that the society is the root cause in the origin of good and evil. He says if a man starts behaving immorally, the cause must be looked for in the society. In fact, children will grow accordingly, what we feed to them. Hence, all the formal and informal agencies of education have the responsibility to maintain the value system of our nation.

The primary aim of education should be to give spiritual and moral training to the mind so that it purifies, perfects, strengthens and rejuvenates the mind and enriches the intellect, all of which ultimately help form the foundation for a successful life. The material we feed into the mind during the process of education must create an indomitable spirit which alone will in turn develop a spirit of enquiry, an element of intelligence, an ardent desire for knowledge and understanding supplemented by a social consciousness and anxiety to utilise what they have learnt for the betterment of the society. Schools and colleges, in the real sense, are bound to foster the values among the students. To make education worthy to be granted, its role must be concentrated on guiding and inculcating values among students. The educational programmes need to be carefully planned and implemented so that these values may be internalized and personalized by the students.

REFERENCE

1. Balan K : Education for excellence, Intellectual Publishing House, New Delhi.
2. Hayman Ronald : Nietzsche-A Critical Life, Weiden Field and Nicolson, London.
3. Jaspers Karl : Man in the Modern Age; George Rouledge & Sons Ltd. London, 1933.
4. Jaspers Kari : The idea of University; London 1959.
5. Marcel Gabriel : The Mystery of being : Faith and Reality; Univ. press of New York, London.
6. Ready V. Narayan Karan : Man, Education and Values; B.R. Publishing Corporation, New Delhi.
7. Sri Aurobindo : Superman; Arya Publishing House, Calcutta, 1944.
8. Sri Aurobindo : Man slave or free; 1966.
9. Sterm J.P. : A Study of Nietzsche; Cambridge Univ. Press.
10. Stewart David : Exploring the philosophy of Religion; Prentice Hall. Inc. Englewood. Cliffs AJ 07632.
11. Strong Tracy B : Friedrich Nietzsche and the Politics in Transfiguration; Univ. of California Press, Los Angeles, London.
12. Sorely : Moral Values and the Idea of God.

10
Future Concerns for Value Education

Gyanendra Nath Tiwari

These days there is so much preference of inculcating values in people; and of course, there is an urgent need to do so. But we find that even those who talk of spreading values are not clear as to what these values are. For example, people know hardly much about social justice, equality, secularism, democracy, etc. The term 'value' itself connotes different meaning to different people (Rokeach. 1973). Values have been referred to as beliefs about desirable ways of behaving or being or having value for particular actions or life style, object, etc. values are also referred to as broad qualities that underline and justify attitudes and behaviours (Schwartz., 1996). Although values have been classified differently by different people, these classifications are highly tentative and overlapping. Values also differ with respect to the motivational goals they express. Meaning of values exists in their empirical relationship with the other values.

More than the listing of values or their classification it is the process of valuing or acquisition of values which is more important (Yuktananda 1989). Since values are beliefs, like all beliefs they have cognitive, affective and behavioural aspects (Rokeach 1973). It is in this valuing process that the educators is similar to the process of problem solving and decision making which involve pinning down the specific problem of questions relating to value-collection of information about its weighing information, accepting or rejecting the position taken.

Mode of Value Education:

Ancient Indian education had always been loaded with value components. The education upto eighteenth century involved study of scriptures and Upanishads, which are heavily loaded with the discourses on morality, ethics and virtuosity. The value education was the pivotal concern around which other knowledge areas are woven.

Later the influences of culture from across the boundaries and British colonization brought about changes in the structure of society. The urban living replaced village symbiotic existence, joint family gave way to unitary family and consequent changes sneaked into the school ethos unwarranted. Apart from these developments simultaneously growing influence of science and technology and consequent industrialization led to efforts aimed at strengthening of the education system by increasing inputs and technology. However, in the process of modernization of education the emphasis shifted to economic and secular values. The education system lost its role as a guardian of ethical and moral values. The detachment of education from its ethical and moral character and introduction of piecemeal topics is curriculum did not bring about any desirable improvements in respect of affective and social outcomes rather it led to deterioration. These developments were not unknown to those concerned with planning and execution of educational policies. The efforts are continuing to reconstruct education to fulfil its role in preservation of the moral character of the society and to keep pace with the economic and technological development.

Changing pattern of Values:

Values changed with the change of concerns and demands from time to time. In ancient times, idealistic values were emphasized over other values. Truth, Goodness and Beauty were considered as eternal values and the whole system of education centered on it. As time changes naturalistic values emphasized on the importance of nature, natural balance, conservation of natural resources etc., *i.e.* the main concern was concerned with self-gratification. Humanistic philosophy laid emphasis on importance of human being and its development in all respect. But now-a-days erosion of values is a matter of concern to all those concerned with education. It is not only in India that deterioration in human values has attracted the concern of educationists, a lot of attention is being given in this respect at international level too (Nanzhao, 1996).

Modern Value system:

Shrinking of the distance across the globe brought about by the developments in the area of science and technology like satellites and Internets have made the world much smaller place enhancing the interactive communication potential. The communication and interface across boundaries of nation leads to increased awareness of their cultural identities. Heightened awareness of the cultural identities and the concerns for preservation of the cultural value system has aroused different reactions, the melting pot theory of kisinger, the rise of fundamentalism, and other racial encounters across the continents. The conflicts of interests are the symptoms of insecurity regarding the preservation of values people subscribe values to this insecurity regarding their cultural values and identities prompts action to ensure the preservation of their own traditional value. Social cohesion may become a casualty as a result of this insecurity, which is gripping ethnic groups all over the world.

The other factor that has an impact on the value system, is the growing economic liberalism, which has failed to benefit all equally. In order to bring about harmonious development of human race all over the world and equal sharing of the resources, social development has to keep pace with economic, scientific and technological progress. Uneven social development, both within and outside nations, has created pockets of discontentments and tensions over sharing and controlling of resources. The lure of the lands associated with advanced and developed cultures has created elitist impatient and intolerant groups concerned with progress at all costs. The crises precipitated by the conflicts prevailing in different societies between the old cultural values handed down through generations and the present demands of scientific and technological worldviews has to be averted. In order to make it possible, the indigenous traditional values have to be examined and innovated (Nanzhao, 1996). So as to play a positive role in concurrent global social-economic context. Otherwise, the next generation might disown not only the incompatible values but also the total cultural value system. Retrieving the baby from bath-water will entail conferring distinction on it, i.e. distinguishing the shared contextually relevant values from the non-functional social goals (Parker, Ninomya and Cogan, 1999). This is not an easy task in the midst of the religious, racial and cultural diversity of present decade. In spite of the challenges, there is urgency to take care of these differences so as to create an environment of mutual respect where all would get equal opportunity to share resources and development.

Future concerns for value education:

Concluding this discussion we can find out future concerns of value education. Swami Vivekananda believed, "The idea of all education, all training should be man-making, education is not the amount of information that is put into your brain and runs riot there undigested all you life, we must have life building, man-making, character-making assimilation of ideas."

Looking at the future of mankind, there is a mixed feeling. While we are striving for a better global economic and social order, there are numerous hardcore problems created by us throughout the passage of history. World over societies are witnessing, widening economic disparities among and within the countries, mounting debt burden, rapid population growth, widespread environmental degradation, civil strife and armed conflict, political turmoil, poverty and what is worst, total value deterioration. Therefore, proper and formal value education is the need of the day. Any effort regarding value education in future should concentrate on following points.

(*i*) Our main objective should be to inculcate values at the early formative years of an individual so that they start developing into integrated personalities blossoming mentally, emotionally, intellectually and spiritually.

(*ii*) Promotion of eternal values and creation of a proper environment in educational institutions to inculcate these among students the future citizens should be given top priority. In the entire educational system, intellect and intuition, science and spirituality, living and learning have to be promoted in a balanced manner.

(*iii*) The curriculum planner should carefully adopt a well-defined approach to achieve the objectives of value inculcation during the course of curriculum transaction at various stages of school education. A broad framework of value orientation may emphasize upon:

1. ***Personal Values:*** Related to physical mental and moral structure.
2. ***Social Values:*** Which may include relations with peer groups, elders and society at large.
3. ***National Values:*** May include in developing sense of patriotism, tolerance and good citizenship.
4. ***Heritage Values:*** Which may emphasis upon the developments of achievement, knowledge of art, craft, music and history.
5. ***International or global values:*** Which may cover the development of scientific temper, issues related to environment and its protection.

(*iv*) Schools through their various activities should make a deliberate attempt for propagating the desired and cherished values for the holistic development of an individual. There can be various methods and techniques achieving this. In order to optimize learning, it is desirable that one teacher should not teach values as a distinct subject but through various disciplines and innovative methods which permeate various subjects. Some specific and direct programmes in the school timetable, for example the school assembly, curricular and co-curricular activities, celebration of religious festivals, team games and sports, social service programme can all help in promoting cooperation, mutual regard, honesty and integrity, discipline and social responsibility at an early age. The activities can be designed from primary to university level keeping in view the physical and psychological development of students at various levels.

(*v*) Real, good and dedicated teachers who are able to provide proper overall guidance to the students should be identified, professionally trained, promoted and provided appropriate economic status, which will attract the best and most talented persons to the noble-teaching programme, the teachers are introduced to the concept of value development and also made aware of methods and techniques keeping in view the physical and psychological development of the student to promote human values. It is important to develop the vision of the teachers in such a way that they can incorporate suitable strategies and methods while teaching any subject, be it science of humanities.

In a world of LPG, i.e. liberalization, privatization and globalization each nation of world is interlinked, therefore, it is imperative for all the nations of the world to live in harmony and create synergy. Only then a true sense of humanity can be visualized in each individual. In this great effort a proper value education can work efficiently.

REFERENCES

Khandelwal, B.P. (1999) : Values for Human Excellence, Journal of Indian Education, New Delhi.

Nanzhao, J.R., (2000) : Introduction of Education and Culture for Economic and Human Development: An Asian Perspective, In Delors J. (Ed.) Learnings: The Treasure within - France: UNESCO

Pant, D. (2000) : Conceptual Aspects of Value Education, Journal of Indian Education, New Delhi.

Parker. W. L., Ninomya, A and Cogen, J (1999): Educating World Citizens; Towards Multinational Curriculum Development, American Educational Research Journal, 36 (2), pp-117-145.

Rokeach, M (1973); The Nature of Human Value, New York: The Free Press.

11
Values and Holistic Approach in Education

Bimla Verma
Ritu Garg

In ancient India, the instruction of a teacher (guru) to a student (disciple) would start as follows:

"Let your conduct be marked by right action, including studies and the teaching of the scriptures; by truthfulness and word, deed and thought; by self-denial and the practice of austerity; by poise and self-control; by performance of the everyday duties of life with a cheerful heart and in unattached mind. Deviate not from the path of good."

From the end of eighteenth century, the rise of academies and polytechnics had expanded the traditional concept of educational institutions and universities as the place for mainly humanistic studies, to cover provision for skills to explore resource potential, to produce goods and services to negotiate terms of transaction and to manage material wealth. The value system had changed too and became "the criteria used by the members of the society to evaluate objects, ideas, acts, feelings or events as to their relative desirability, merit or correctness". Individual freedom and material progress also became important values in life.

Towards the close of the twentieth century, several important changes have occurred in human life all over the world, which require special attention with a view to redefining values on an international scale. Development of communication and information technology has made the world a global village and has given rise to issues of justice, equity, freedom, democracy and human rights. Rejection of the communist ideology has brought about ethnic conflicts, nationalism and religious fanaticism. Greed for material progress has broken limits.

With the rapid escalation of social changes, especially in the last two decades, our educational system has many issues that need to be resolved. It is the awesome responsibility of each generation to pass on the torch of civilization to the next. The present scenario in our country is really a cause of concern and should be tackled with immediate effect.

In ancient India, education was primarily value oriented, however, the so-called modern education is unable to respond to the most crucial purpose of education, that is, character-building through inculcation of universal human values. On the contrary, there has been an erosion of values on a continuing basis. Whether a child shall grow up to regard life with suspicion or with confidence; to be deceitful or straight forward; contentious and grasping or co-operative and loyal. These and other characteristics are determined by the treatment he receives and obviously they enter into the essential qualities of spiritual life in general and of his religion in particular.

In the outer world of bitter competition and immoral strife, each one of us is compelled to battle constantly with things and beings. Deep within ourselves also, we have become helpless slaves to our uncontrollable desires and undisciplined thoughts. Thus, the modern man/child comes to be torn between two forces, the objective tensions and the subjective confusions. In our experiences in life, we fall into detestable environments and distressing circumstances, which provoke and enrage us weakening our inner personality. In our day to day experiences in the so-called civilized and modern society, most of our actions seem to emanates from the realm of our mind and we are misled by feelings instead of being guided by our intellectual discrimination. But religion helps us keep our intellect alert and apply its faculty of discrimination to the choice of right action at every moment of our life.

Today's children are under pressure to be smart, to be popular, to become star debaters or athletes and to achieve these successes they are under constant stress. Education is one of the major areas where special pressure is placed on our children without realizing the different levels of potential in each child. The materialism in society makes the child realise that it can remove the agony of poverty, the sorrows of illness and the discomforts of a limited life. But spirituality and philosophy indicate that in spite of the highest standard of living, man cannot feel happy in his ambitions and live contented in his relationships with others merely because he has plenty of food, clothing shelter and all other amenities of a peaceful and efficient national life.

Development of biotechnology and bio-informatics, etc. has brought about, on the one hand increased agricultural production, better medical facilities, some environmental gains, but has also created problems of 'gene cloning' and 'surrogate motherhood', raising complex ethical issues. These considerations lead us to the re-articulation of the need for values-based education in the twenty-first century.

While the basic values of seeking the truth, practicing honesty and appreciating beauty, remain intact, secular values like tolerance, self-respect, lover for human dignity, respect and compassion for others, individual freedom and human rights, internationalism, rejection of cruelty, the practice of non-violence and the culture of peace have become more important today because of the problems facing the human race described above.

Since educational policies can contribute to the development of understanding, solidarity and tolerance among individuals and among ethnic, social, cultural and religious groups, education can be the main instrument to promote knowledge, values, attitudes and skills conducive to respect for human rights and to build a culture of peace democracy.

The "Integrated framework of Action" carried out Director General of UNESCO in Nov. 1995, emphasised the development in every individual a sense of universal values and types of behaviour on which a culture of peace can be predicted. Education, as it was emphasised, must develop the ability to val·ıe freedom and the skills to meet its challenges; it must develop the ability to recognize and accept the values which exist in the diversity of individuals, genders, peoples and cultures and develop the ability to communicate, share and co-operate with others; it must develop the ability of non-violent conflict resolution and promote the development of inner peace in the minds of students so that they can establish firmly the qualities of tolerance, compassion, sharing and caring; It must cultivate in citizens the ability to make informal choices; it must teach citizens to respect the cultural heritage, protect the environment, adopt methods of production and consumption leading to sustainable development with harmony between individuals and collective values between immediate basic needs and long term interests. And finally it must cultivate feelings of solidarity and equity at the national and international levels. Strategies to achieve these aims and the lines of action in respect of the content, teaching materials and resources. Programmes of reading, expression and the promotion of foreign languages, educational establishments, training of teachers, action on behalf of vulnerable groups, research and development, higher education, co-ordination between the education sector and other agents of socialisation, regional and international co-operation, have been designed for the use of the members states of UNESCO to promote education for peace, human rights and democracy.

Value-based education has become center-stage in recent efforts of the Government of India to re-orient the education system. The National Resource Centre on Value Education (NRCVE) was set up at NCERT as an outcome of strategic planning to realize the objectives of values-based education at school stage in the country.

Value-education and a holistic approach in education will enable us to learn in life to discriminate between serious and trifling, the permanent and the impermanent, the full and the empty occupations, and employ our precious life span in seeking and striving to acquire the lasting, the full happiness and the glory of a community.

REFERENCES

Gupta, N.L., Human Value in Education, Concept Publishing Company, New Delhi.

Sharma, Y.K., Foundations in Sociology of Education, Kanishka Publishers, New Delhi.

Sharma, S.R. (1998) Shiksha Evam Vidya, Akhand Jyoti Sansthan, Mathura.

12
Values And Global Society

N. Shamshi
Manju Rani

A value is something that pervades everything. It determines the meaning of the world as a whole as well as the meaning of every person, every event and every action. Even the smallest change introduced into the world by some agent has a value and is undertaken only on the ground and for the sake of some value moments. Everything that exists or even everything that may exist is of such nature that it not only exists but also contains written itself either the justification or in confirmation of its being. It can be said of everything that it is either good or bad, it can be said whether it must be or must not be. This is the broad view in respect of values expressed by Lockesky and Marshall.

Let us review, briefly what values imply to the common man. When I ask a question "Which susbstance is heavier lead or iron?" I am dealing with the realm of ascertainable facts in which universally accepted standards are available. The pronouncement here might be called factual judgement. If, however, I ask "which of the two pictures is more beautiful or where in the country is the best place to live in?" I face a question not of fact but of value. Thinking here involves a process of evaluation which is closely related to my desires and interests. Value has to be experienced. There are three opinions as to the nature of values:—

(*a*) Values are objective they exist in the world of nature—they are biological. A value may be defined as a quality in objects on situations that calls forth appreciation or preference.

(*b*) Values are subjective i.e. they belong wholly to the realm of mind they are psychological. Value judgements vary from person to person and from age to age. The values which a thing seems to have arise from its satisfaction of some desires and interest.

Values are both subjective and objective. They are products of interaction between variables: (*i*) a person, (*ii*) an environmental situation. Value is objective to the extent that it is a personal judgement with a pronounced emotional one. A value is a relationship between a person and an environmental situation which evokes appreciative response in the individual.

It does not matter whether values lie within the realm of ethics, economics, lie within the realm of ethics, economics, aesthetics or religion, the important thing is that are experienced in the human minds and are translated into human action and it is a widely accepted fact that they substantially determine an individual's likes and dislikes and largely controls his behaviour. Stein described values as the choice men make and the ends they live by.

Values determine the intensity and continuity of a particular human behaviour. If a high value is attached to a particular idea or feeling it instigates and directs behaviour with considerable force. Conversely an idea or feeling of trivial value attached to it will have little force in directing behaviour. Hence, generally speaking, we can say that values are the key choices that shape the type of life that an individual carves out himself and the kind of person he becomes.

Today, we are at the crossroads of a value crisis. It is period of value lag, old values have eroded and new values are yet to stylise. Something seems to have gone wrong tragically with the course of events in the past century and some factors stand out as contributory to the value crisis:

We are living in a period of rapid change. We have changed within a few generations from a society predominantly rural and simple in organisation to a highly industrialised machine civilization which is becoming increasingly interdependent and impersonal. The industrial technological and atomic revolutions are producing a society which is mechanically efficient but which threatens to destroy itself. The danger is that we have learned how to split the atom before we have learned how to write mankind.

There is a precariousness about life, a vague manners. War in this century could spell annibihilation of mankind.

Terrorism has become a global threat, a subversive creed ushering in a cult of violence.

The growth of the mass media of communication is having a profound effect on manners and morals. A generation ago the home church (religion) and schools were the main institutions in establishing and re-informing moral standards and social patterns. Today motion pictures. TV, newspapers, magazines are largely taking over these functions. The situation has become highly complicated by exposure to unwholesome programmes on TV, cable, video films and internet which are full of crime, violence and acts of terrorism.

Disparity, dissension, communal tensions, violence in the name of politics and religion have permeated within human society threatening to tear apart the fabric of global society.

Our temples of learning are vitiated by drug addictions-alcoholism and vandalism. In these days of nucleus families, children are a neglected lot with parents having no time to spare for them. With both parents working, the children have to find for themselves on return from school. The parents are so busy with their social life, professions and economic pressures that the parent-child relationship and rapport has greatly weakened. Family discord and tensions have increased broken homes, separated and divorced parents, single parent homes have all led to special emotional problems for the children.

Money or culture and materialism have taken over in a big way and wholesome values have been left behind. Statistics shows that the majority of crimes—robberies, murders, burglaries, acts of violence and terrorism are committed teenagers, college and school dropouts and young adults.

It feels to an imperative statement that teachers should become the role models to their pupils. Qualities and values which are to be inculcated in the child have to be found in the teachers. Values of teachers influence the values of the institutional social system. Blackington indicated "which value will be influenced or transmitted depends upon the teacher's own value-orientation." This leads us to the importance of value education which means the proper development of values, attitudes, feelings and behaviour patterns which cut across all our curricular experiences, instructions of which is to be planned systematically and to be implemented properly. The recommendation made in the National Policy of Education 1986 on value education reads thus "The growing concern over the erosion of essential values and an increasing agnicism in the society has brought to focus the need for readjustment in the curriculum in order to make education forceful tool for the cultivation of social and moral values."

In our culturally plural global society, education should foster universal and eternal-values oriented towards the unity and integration of our people. Such value education should help eliminate obscurantism, religious fanatism, violence, superstition and fatalism.

In the words of Pandit Jawahar Lal Nehru, "An university stands for humanism for tolerance, for reason, for the adventure of ideas and for the search of truth. It stands for forward march of human race towards even higher objectives."

REFERENCES

Kaur, Tripat (2004) Values and Ethics in Management, Galgotia Publishing Company, New Delhi.

Passi, B.K & Singh Prabhakar (2004) Value Education, Rakhi Prakashan 6/9 H.I.G Flats, Sanjay Place, Agra.

Buch. M.B (1988-1992) Fifth Survey of Educational Research vol. II

Dissertation Abstracts Internationals - 1990 [vol. 51 no. 6].

13
Human Values and Technical Education Need, Expectations and Challenges

Navneet Arora

This article is not meant to tell something new to you. But if it may help discover the human values hidden within you and boost a bit to live for those values then the very purpose of the article is achieved. These are human values without which the selfishness and corruption are becoming parts of every system and we all are its victims. We are waiting in queue for our turn, if not victimised so far. The human values, the supreme need of today's world, can play a vital role in the development of total personality of our youth and thus whole world. The paper repeats the known facts' viz. the human behaviour, need of morality, value education, values to be inculcated among students various activities to be persuaded and responsibilities to inculcated among students, various activities to be persuade and responsibilities to be shared. Why this whole revision exercise? Answer is simple. Just to remind you that the goodness is within you, explore it and become role models for others.

Introduction

Education should cease to denote merely intellectual development or gathering information about different subjects. Education should mean the development of man's total personality. According Dr. R.N. Tagore, '**The highest education**

is that which does not merely give us information but makes our life in harmony with all other existences.' Education can play this responsibility if value education becomes its part and parcel.

Education needs a total reform with an emphasis on Value-based Education to produce sensible educated youth. Otherwise it is rightly said, 'We human beings are moral cannibals feeding upon each other's misfortunes.' Without morality and self-knowledge, the scientific knowledge is being used to create weapons and the world is spending millions of dollars every minute upon arms. Some one has said rightly, 'Accursed is the race of homo-sapiens because they kill in plenty and they kill their own kind'.

Advancement and worldly progress without development of higher feelings in man's heart is causing hell on the earth itself. Few years back there was a cartoon in English daily showing two inhabitants of moon talking in panic about the menace of man reaching or invading the moon, meaning thereby that man has created hell on the earth and now he will create a similar one on the moon. Education based on Values is the need of the hour.

Linguistic fanaticism, communal fanaticism, caste fanaticism and regional fanaticism have become parts of our character. Not only uneducated masses but also the so-called educated and super-intelligent men are indulged in fanaticism, corruption, selfishness, slow self-suicide and personality degrading activities like smoking, drinking and drugs, etc.

Solution to these problems lies in imparting Value-based Education to new generations. Few questions are arisen : What is to Morality? What should be the programme for this mission? How to impart it? Who is capable of imparting it? This paper helps give an insight to these questions.

2. VALUE ORIENTED EDUCATION

2.1 Need

So many thinkers in our country no less than our government realize the sad consequences of education without moral and spiritual instructions.

The defect with our system of education is that it lacks national culture. It does not help evolve national sentiments or patriotism in the educated.

There are scholars in our country who do not like anything in the culture of their country and who consider every thing foreign as good. How sad it is!

Efforts are to be made to have management and the educators who have cultivated moral and spiritual life in themselves and who can bless students by the holy influences of their moral life. We need value oriented to produce great teachers first.

2.2 Philosophy of Human Personality

The study of human behaviour should be the primary object of study of morality and religion. The scientific methodology is the best tool. All metaphysical interpretations of soul as unborn, eternal, unchanging and capable of disembodied existence are to be rejected. Mythical wings of soul are to be clipped and installed it in natural world. It is painstaking study of human psyche through method.

We should accept the biological truth that man, both in his body and soul, has evolved from one of the species of chimpanzee. So human psyche has natural origin. Individual psyche has its origin in the coalescence of the sperm and the ovum. Again, individual consciousness or psyche exists in indissoluble relation with body so that it ceases to exist, if body dies. Human psyche is part of the natural order, is born and is subject to change, growth, decay and death. Human soul has dependent origination, life and death.

Good is understandable as good of the soul. Intrinsic good is good of the soul . The laws of the soul are the moral laws. The course of conduct which degrades and diseases the soul is evil principle of conduct. Good and bad in moral sense are concerned with the health and disease of the psyche or soul.

Value oriented education would also include and teach the condition in which human soul damages, degrades, diseases and debilitates itself. Take tasty dishes. A man finds some dish too tasty. He takes more of it than his stomach can stand. By overeating he damages his bodily health. If he again overeats, even when he knows that it harms his health, he does not realize that his soul has grown weak to resist the risk of ill health or death.

Take the case of sex satisfaction. There are biological and social conditions in which its satisfaction is healthy. But if the pleasure of sex satisfaction gets the better of a person and he indulges in sex satisfaction knowing that it ruins the innocence of a girl or fidelity of a married woman or respect of his wife and indulges in it in spite of himself, his indulgence has weakened his soul to resist doing harm to himself and society.

Take a third example, I feel pleasure in earning money. However, if the pleasure of earnings gets better of me and I see how I gain money by cheating others, knowing that cheating is an evil and untruthful for me and others, my soul gets weaker and weaker to resist in doing harm to itself and others.

Good and bad are qualities of conduct in relation to self and others. They are not divinely determined. Evil or sin is not violation of the command of God. What is pious or good is not what pleases God. Good and bad have nothing to do with pleasure or displeasure of God.

Good and bad are not matter of punishment and reward by God. Good conduct is conducive to the health of the soul, as nutritive food is conducive to the health of the body. Bad conduct damages, degrades, debilitates and diseases the soul as taking of indigestible or poisonous food damages the life of the body.

Let us further make clear as to what is meant by diseased state of soul. If an intemperate man knows that over-indulgence in food, drinks and sex is evil for him and others and yet does not find strength enough to avoid them, his soul is diseased for it cannot resist evil to himself and others. Again, if in order to satisfy his intemperance or greed, he indulges in falsehood to get his satisfaction, his soul is diseased. So a soul is diseased if it indulges in what is evil and untruthful. There is casual relation between the values of goodness and truth and life.

They are conditions for health, strength and longevity of soul.

In a nutshell, if one's soul is healthy then the thoughts and actions would be positive, moral and value- oriented.

2.3 Symptoms of Morality?

Morality means good health of soul. How we can judge the goodness in others or us? The answer is:

1. To Be Good is to Feel Related
2. To Be Good is to Feel Concerned
3. To Be Good is to Be Affectionate
4. To Be Good is to Seek Harmony
5. To Be Good is to Have Reverence
6. To Be Good is to Have Gratitude
7. To Be Good is to Make Amends
8. To Be Good is to Feel Related
9. To Be Good is to Respect to Other Existences
10. To Seek Harmony is to Cultivate Altruistic Feelings

3. GUIDELINES FOR VALUE EDUCATION PLANNING

A value education program in our curriculum should be added. For which the syllabus can be framed on the basis of detailed list of various value given below. Value-based Education can inculcate innumerable values among students and society. Few of them can be classified as follows:

(A) Self Oriented Values

1. Self Knowledge
2. Self Sufficiency
3. Self Control
4. Self Education
5. Self Discipline
6. Self Esteem
7. Self Confidence
8. Self Appraisal
9. Self Sacrifice
10. Self Transcendence
11. Self Analysis
12. Self Criticism

13. Cleanliness-Inner
14. Simplicity
15. Modesty
16. Cleanliness-Environmental
17. Moral Courage
18. Good Health
19. Quick & Correct Decisions
20. Accurate Judgment
21. Adventure
22. Responsible Behaviour
23. Contentment
24. Creativity
25. Punctuality & Consistency
26. Determination
27. Motivation
28. Trustworthiness & Loyalty
29. Systematic Approach
30. Humility

(B) Family Oriented Values

1. Maternal Love
2. Paternal Love
3. Caring and Sharing
4. Co-operation
5. Spirit of Service
6. Harmony and Peace
7. Mutual Trust
8. Chastity
9. Gratitude
10. Mutual Respect
11. Tolerance
12. Reverence

(C) Society Oriented Values

1. Spirit of Total Social Responsibility
2. Spirt of Service and Reform
3. Spirit of Reverence and Gratitude
4. Spirit of Respect for Life

5. Consideration for Rights of Others
6. Spirit of Enthusiastic Performance of Constitutional Duties, Specially Fundamental Duties
7. Love for Noble Social Environment
8. Spirit of Harmony with Human Beings
9. Spirit of Special Service to Benefactors and Elders
10. Faith in Equality, Liberty and Fraternity
11. Faith in Humanism, Social Justice, Democracy and Value Saturated Secularism
12. Power of Oration and Value-oriented Leadership Development
13. Spirit of Cooperation and Healthy Competition
14. Spirit of Missionary Life
15. Spirit of Pride in Composite Culture
16. Reverence for Famous Educationists, Statesmen, Reformers, Scientists, Spiritualists and Patriots
17. Respect for Charters of Human Rights of the child, Rights of Women and the Aged
18. Spirit of Removing Defects and Deficiencies in Society

(D) Nature Oriented Values

1. Love for Knowledge of Nature
2. Willing Obedience to Laws of Nature
3. Development of Scientific Method, Scientific Faith and Belief
4. Love for Understanding Laws of Nature
5. Development of Scientific Temper
6. Spirit of Conservation of Nature
7. Spirit Of Preserving Purity of Nature
8. Compassion for all Living Beings
9. Spirit of Service of all Human Beings, Animals, Birds, Trees and Plants.
10. Good Care of Physical Things
11. Hatred of Polluting Environment
12. Love for Truths and Beauties of Nature

4. RESPONSIBILITIES, CHALLENGES AND ACTIVITIES

4.1 Responsibility As an Educator

The first and foremost question is : **Can there be a moral education without moral educators?** The answer is : **No.** The values listed above should be inculcated in students. Who is responsible for this mission? The answer is 'Education' and 'Educators'. We can imagine the responsibility enjoined upon the education and educators.

If youth is the greatest wealth and pride of a nation, then those who are interested in this wealth have a tremendous responsibility. Can we give the best to the students if we ourselves are the worst, dishonest, greedy, mercenary, materialistic, selfish and vain, devoid of sense of duty, lacking in spirit of service, shorn of humibility, reverence and gratitude and do not have good manners and punctuality, etc.? **There can be no moral education without moral educators.** Hence teachers of high moral caliber are the greatest need of value-oriented education.

4.2 Expectations from Educators

We need educators whose example of noble life the students can emulate, who can inspire the students to become good, noble citizens of the world and to so live their lines that they will help lessen the misery, darkness and conflict of the present world. We teach and preach through lectures, books and seminars, but the real teaching and preaching is done by us by the example of life, by every act and thought, every moment of our life.

Life begets life. A lighted lamp alone can light the other lamp. Hence the need of such teachers who are honest, hard-working, dedicated, chaste, unselfish, humble grateful, respectful, disciplined, punctual and well mannered, who have a missionary zeal and good of students at heart, who do not work only for money – though money should be paid to them adequately – but work with a nobler and higher aim, who deem it their wonderful and proud privilege to play the role of nation builders.

Educational institutions must not turn out rebellious, undisciplined, selfish and irresponsible young men. But how can they do better if there is none to inspire them for a better and nobler life? The teachers must have the caliber to impress the students so that they begin to hate to be drug addict, selfish, chaotic and ungrateful.

4.3 Challenge should be accepted

We may feel that this is expecting too much from the teachers but if we have no higher aim we can have no higher planning and efforts. It will be worthless to impart technical education if it only sharpens the intellect without developing moral qualities.

When these so-called 'Educated youth' become engineers, administrators, contractors, industrialists, officers and politicians etc., will they serve and help their countrymen or exploit them? Will their life and profession become a blessing for others or will they worship only the self?

Education must be higher aim-oriented, higher life-oriented. Imparting value-based education is a challenge in front of the educators and they must accept the same!

4.4 Role of the Parents

It is truly stated, 'Education commences at the mother's knee and every word spoken within the hearsay of little children tends towards formation of character'. The foundations of character of a man are laid in his home. The responsibility is to be equally shared by parents to impart moral values to the youth. What parents expect should first of all practice themselves. If we as parents expect respect from our children, we must pay the same to our elders and benefactors. Our actions are more powerful than words. We should be moral enough so that we may have courage to give a piece of advice to our children. An understanding and cooperation among parents and educators is must to build the character of the nation.

4.5 Activities to be Organised

In order to inculcate moral values amongst the students, the following activities may be organized in the institutions willing to start the value education programme:

1. Parents Day
2. Motherland Day
3. Teacher's Day
4. Humanity Day
5. Animals' Day
6. Blood Donation Camps
7. Eye Donation Campaign
8. Adult Education Programme
9. Service in Slum Areas
10. Seminars/Debates to be organized on the topics of moral and social relevance like : Evils of Caste System, Dowry, Bribery.

Corruption, Ragging, Humanism and the need of human values in life as listed above.

The list of such value- oriented activities can be extended depending on the local needs and the moral calibre of the value educators.

5. CONCLUSIONS

Value-based Education makes our life in harmony with other existences. The youth with moral values becomes blessing to the nation. A unique evolutionary and scientific vision about soul can impart value-based education through moral person. Moral literature and teachings of great men can bring a revolution. The responsibility is on the shoulders of the educators to develop the altruistic feelings and values in their heart and then impart these values in the youth of the nation. The mission is unique but demands a missionary zeal and deep love for selfless service.

REFERENCES

1. P.V. Kanal, Altruism.
2. Dale Karnegi, How to Win Friends and Influence People?
3. Girwar Prasad, Moral, Human and Spiritual Values.
4. Vikas Dev, Moral Education – The Supreme Need.
5. Shiv Khera, You can win
6. Jack Canfield, Soup for the Soul
7. Napolean Hill, Think and Grow Rich
8. Zig Ziglar, Raising Positive Kids in a Negative World
9. John C. Maxwell, The Success Journey
10. S.P. Kanal, To Be Good.

14
Value Inculcation—Holistic Approach in Education

Rachna Verma Mohan

Education is a process which helps the individual attain a satisfied and harmonious life in society. The right type of education can bring about social transformation, economic growth and modernization leading to national development as the main purpose of education is to build up a healthy society and development of values among students. As Education Commission (1964-66) pointed out, "It is essential to transform the system of education qualitatively in terms of its value content, standard and relevance to life. The role of education to promote humanistic outlook, sense of brotherhood and a commitment to ethical and cultural values needs to be re-emphasized."

Nature of Values

Allport (1969) has defined value as "a belief upon which a man acts by preferences." Values are patterns of choices that guide persons of groups towards satisfaction and fulfilment. Values impart significance to life. They are enduring beliefs which work as motivational set, and force the individual to respond in a specific manner based on socially and culturally approved preferences and judgement. They are guiding principles of life. Values help us not in self-evaluation, but in self drive too. They are considered as potent determinants of human behaviour.

Value Education

Education that helps in discriminating between what is right and wrong, proper and improper in thought and action of an individual about an object, event or situation, may be termed as value education. It develops positive attitude and constructive approach in our day-to-day activities. It is through education that the society seeks to preserve and promote its values aiming at all round development of the learner's personality.

Need of Value-Oriented Education

India has its own cultural heritage right from the ancient Gurukul system. The development of character constituted a significant aspect of education. Besides mental training was emphasized to a great extent. In Gurukuls/Ashrams rigorous character training was given to the students. They were required to follow strict discipline and code of moral conducts. Value inculcation was the main aim of the education. But today education is mostly concerned with the acquisition of knowledge and passing of examinations in order to achieve economic gains. Value development which is necessary for building up an integrated and morally matured person is not getting due attention. Access to white collar jobs with monetary and other perks has become the ultimate concern of our students without any care for development of character. A positive attitude towards life is lacking. Negative passions like hatred, violence and a sense of frustration and insecurity are visible everywhere.

Present day education, is so organized as to deliberately destroy virtue which is a state of mind or consciousness in which there is love, compassion and humility. The aim and vision of education system is to produce an ambitious, aggressive, successful man. Education has been considered as a means of cultivating power and economic development. The whole purpose of education, at present, is to produce bright engineers, doctors, computer scientists, etc. Value development has been completely neglected in the process of education. There is no humility, no cooperation, no harmony. In this reference P. Krishna (1999) stated, "There is competition, rivalry, ambition and the race for success from which violence arises in order to dominate and be at the top. That is the kind of man we are producing and then we complain that there is too much violence in the society and governments are not able to control it and we need a better police force and the army should be sent in there to control this and so on. But what is it that we are doing at the source from where all this originates?"

Education no more manifests the inner qualities of man. There is congruence between his outer actions and inner feelings. This loss of congruence results in loss of character and consequent erosion of values in various walks of life. It is the task. This harmony can only be achieved through a purposive effort in the form of development of values. In order to fulfil this purpose value inculcation should get an important place in the content of education. The purpose of education then would be to reveal to a human being, child of adult, all that is beautiful in life. There is great beauty in life, in friendship, in art, dance and music. Education must produce a mind that is inquiring, learning, growing inwardly, having awareness of values in life.

Some Efforts in the Area of Value Education

After independence various commissions and committees emphasized the need for inculcation of values and provision for value education in schools. The first commission appointed after independence of the country, namely the University Education Commission (1948-49) considers the issue of inculcation of religious and moral values, in the educational context at the university stage. It stated "we must habituate the students to right emotion, induce in them the formation of good moral, mental and physical habits. Only what one accepts willingly becomes a part of oneself. In the early stages, the books should contain not only moral lessons but lives of great men given as things of supreme human interest, lives which exemplify the living of great thought and noble emotions." The Secondary Education Commission (1952-53) was of the view that the attitudes, values and modes of behaviour of the society are bound to be reflected in the school as it is a smaller society. There may be indiscipline in the society but the school has to take the responsibility of its removal from the society. The commission feels it is the responsibility of the head master and teachers to set a high standard of work conduct. The activities of the school should be planned to create congenial environment for training of right character. The purpose of education is fulfilled only if certain definite values are inculcated in the minds of the youth of the country.

The Committee on Religious and Moral Instruction (1959) headed by Shri Prakash recommended, "we are not unaware of the various steps that are being taken at different educational levels towards literacy drive, adult education and education of the handicapped. If the content of education is also enriched with moral and spiritual values, the purpose of education, will have been truly fulfilled." The Education Commission (1964-66) recommended, "Apart from education in such values being made an integral part of school programme. Generally some period should be set apart in the time table for this purpose."

The National Policy of Education (1986) stressed for readjustment of curriculum for the cultivation of social and moral values. Report of the Committee (1992) for Review of National Policy on Education (1986) recommended "Education must further provide a climate for the nurture of values, both as a personalized set of values forming one's character, and including necessarily social, cultural and national values, so as to have a context and meaning for actions and decisions, in order to enable the persons to act meaning for actions and decisions, in order to enable the persons to act with conviction and commitment." These recommendations have not been implemented properly so far. So holistic approach in education for inculcation of values is required.

Holistic Approach in Education for Value Inculcation

Holistic approach in education should be adopted for imparting values. For this purpose following measures can be taken:

1. Value education should be viewed as an objective of

education rather than area of education. Such education should be defined in clearly identifiable terms and value education should relate both personal and social well being.

2. Value education should develop greater insight into people's feelings, needs and interests. Many aspects of school life can foster such an insight. The study of literature and the other art-creative writing, drama, etc. all can contribute to this end.
3. Many good things are already available in our syllabi and text books, and teachers have to be told how to use them to inculcate right values among students.
4. Teacher training programme should be organized to make teachers aware of various methods and techniques of developing values in the students. They should also promote secular values, equality before law, equality of gender and nurture love for a national identity.
5. Value education should permeate all aspects of school life as well as the curriculum.
6. School should provide curricular and co-curricular activities and experiences inside and outside the classroom which promote responsibility, cooperation, equality, honesty and self-control.
7. These activities should be organized in such a way that they bring together students of various religious, cultures and economic strata.
8. Value discussion be incorporated into the school curriculum.
9. Children in school in the impressionable age of adolescence, should be exposed to the tales and biographies of heroes, of those who stood alone and opposed injustice, cruelty, superstitions, social evils like sati, communal frenzy, etc.
10. All teachers should be regarded as teachers of value education, though some teachers can play a special role in it, because of their awareness, understanding and commitment to the cause.

11. Teachers should try to develop in their students an attitude that the feelings, needs and interests of other people are as important as their own.
12. Teachers should avoid imposing a definite point of view on their students. They should discuss pros and cons of the problem-related values and allow the students to take their own decision. In this way risk of indoctrination can be avoided.
13. Teachers should perceive themselves as role models whose values, attitudes and behaviour have an impact on the development of their students.
14. Value education can be given through content areas also. Every teacher should be able to locate the values inherent in his teaching subject. He should relate that value with day-to-day life experiences of the students. They may be asked to react regarding the applicability of this students. They may be asked to react regarding the applicability of this value in their thoughts and actions.

In the end we can say that by adopting holistic approach in education for value inculcation we can easily develop values in our students. Efforts should be done by society, teachers and every person concerned with the welfare and progress of the nation.

REFERENCES

1. Agarwal, U., 'Some Concerns about Teacher Education, Teacher Education,' IATE, 1998, vol. XXXII, Nos 1&2.
2. Allport, G.W., Vernon, P.E. & Lindsey, G. (1969) 'A Study of Values'; Boston, Haughton Miffin.
3. Gupta, K.M., (1989), 'Moral Development in School Children', The Academic Press, Haryana.
4. Krishna, P. (1999), 'Right Living in Modern Society'; The Theosophical Publishing House, Adyar, Chennai.
5. National Policy on Education, (1986) Government of India, MHRD, Department of Education, New Delhi.
6. 'NCTE Initiatives for Quality Improvement in Teacher Education

Programmes', (2001), NCTE, New Delhi.

7. Programme of Action, (1992) Government of India, M.H.R.D, Department of Education, New Delhi.
8. Report of the University Education Commission, (1948-49), Government of India, Ministry of Education, New Delhi.
9. Report of the Secondary Education Commission, (1952-53), Government of India, Ministry of Education, New Delhi.
10. Report of the Committee on Religious and Moral Instruction, (1959). Report of Moral Education Committee, 1983, U.P.
11. Report of Education Commission (1964-66) Government of India, Ministry of Education, New Delhi.

15
Education in Human Values

Mudita Bhatnagar
Reena Saxena

Values are attributes that spring from the sublimity of soul. They are sentiments which involve mind, feeling and will which are strong and deep. They are like beauty perfections which are not obstructed by any kind of prejudice. They are attitudes that confer on man humanism and peace. In short, values shape the moral personality of an individual. They help him live harmoniously and graciously with his fellowmen.

It can be said -

Values are concept that conserve life.
Values are concept that comfort life.
Values are concept that promote life.
Values are concept that protect life.

Values are indeed the divine side of man. Values give meaning and strength to a person's character by occupying a central place in his life. They reflect one's judgement, behaviour, decisions, choices, dreams, relationships and vision. They guide us to do the right things. They give direction and firmness to life and bring joy, satisfaction and peace to life. We can say that values are like the rails that keep a train on the track and help it move smoothly, quickly and with direction.

Reasons for the Decline of Values

Today, people especially the young are confused about their values and value system. They are facing value conflicts and dilemmas.

The basic reasons for the decrease of values are-

(*i*) Dramatic and far-reaching socio-cultural and political changes.

(*ii*) Breakdown of traditional values without proper replacement.

(*iii*) Conflicting ideologies.

(*iv*) Double standards practised by people in position of power and influence.

In the absence of values, the people have no principle or foundation on the basis of which they can face life situations, make choices and decisions . A life without proper values is chaotic and disastrous and like a rudderless boat.

Good Education

It has main features–

(*i*) Is a man making and character building programme.

(*ii*) Is the training of mind, body and soul.

(*iii*) Is the quest for those nobler aims that integrate culture and technology.

(*iv*) Is the hunt for that goal which liberates man from fear, inertia, ignorance and superstition.

(*v*) It excites passionate hunger for truth.

(*vi*) It aims at perfection and excellence.

(*vii*) It is an instrument of social change and national development.

(*viii*) It moves towards humanism, liberalism and universalism.

(*ix*) It cuts across all narrow barriers that divide man from man.

(*x*) It helps man reach destiny, which is aristocracy of intellect and sublimity of soul.

Value-Oriented Education

Value-oriented education means inculcating in the children a sense of humanism, a deep concern for the well-being of others and the nation. Value-based Education is an encounter with the total personality of the individual keeping in view all aspects of the personality development (moral, social, cultural, spiritual, aesthetic, etc.)

It teaches us to preserve whatever is good and worthwhile in what we have inherited from our culture. It does not mean value imposition or blind imitation.

Value based education has the capacity to transform a diseased mind into a very young, fresh, innocent, healthy, natural and attentive mind. The want of value oriented education has made man money mad, power mad, it's rightly said-

We have passion, but no compassion,
We have goods, but no God,
We have speed, but no direction,
We have production, but no equitable distribution,
We have religion, but no spirituality.

Value-based education involves developing sensitivity to and awareness of what is right, what is good, what is beautiful, ability to choose the right values.

In the words of Swami Vivekanand -

"If you fly in the air,
you are a fly,
If you walk on water,
you are a straw
but if you win the heart of someone,
you are something."

Condition of the Present Society

In the present society, the youth is neither Indian nor Western. They are finding themselves caught in a dilemma. Youth is more concerned with money and not social harmony and social well-being.

Today, we are building a purely economic society. Religion has made us selfish and negligent. We have no regard for public property but we build and protect private property with full regard.

Place of Values in the Present Educational System

The present educational system has mechanistic approach which has added to several problems. It does not give deserving importance to values in human life. The value transition is unhealthy, unpaced or even inharmonious in the content of the role of educational institutions.

"Education without vision is waste;
education without value is crime;
education without mission is life's burden."

The different aims of education - development of the human personality, pursuit of knowledge, preservation of culture, development of character, promotion of social justice, scientific temper, democracy, secularism and so on are just so many varied educational expressions of the constituents of the good life. Education in its aims, curriculum and methods is thus inextricably linked up with values. It is through education that society seeks to preserve and promote its cherished values.

The value based education is an unavoidable necessity. "A nation with atomic power is not a strong nation; but a nation with people with strong character is indeed a strong nation."

Design of Teachers' Training Programmes

There is no magic formula, technique or strategy to inculcate values. Inculcation of values is a life long quest.

The teacher plays a vital role in promoting values. He is a guide, friend and philosopher. Teachers with vision, dealing with curricular activities like NCC, Red Cross, sports and games, field trips, etc. can develop suitable strategies and methods which would enable proper transmission of value.

The curriculum needs to be designed in such a way that an integration is achieved among the theory courses and values are woven with skill dominated and attitude building areas.

The education in human values can help retain humanness, promote purity and thereby help human beings unfold the hidden divinity. The teachers can make a modest beginning by helping and guiding children to keep their school premises clean instilling in them a sense of punctuality and duty.

The teachers can give personal examples as well as the parent-teacher association can unitedly effort to inculcate elementary qualities. Women play an important role in the education of values. She has the capacity not to convert a house into a sweet home but also to transform a country into a strong nation.

Mahatma Gandhi rightly said, "If men are good teachers, women are better teachers."

Values cannot be developed in isolation of one another or even in separate clusters. Educational institutions have to work in a way that the whole children care of. DOING and BEING are more important than KNOWING.

Massages such as the following should be interpreted to develop a belief in the people.

My first duty is to my country.
My second duty is to my parents.
My third duty is to those below me.
My fourth duty is to those above me.
My last duty is to my own gains.

Why Value Education?

For a variety of socio-cultural reasons, the affective objectives of education concerned with the development of feelings, values and attitudes have in recent times suffered serious neglect in our educational institutions.

Education pursued rightly should heighten a person's awareness of oneself and ones relationship with the outside world of nature and other human beings.

We are going through a crisis of values in our social and political life which a special force and point to the entire question of education and value.

The population-increase has seriously affected the quality of life of the masses and has caused social tensions and unrest. Narrow casteist, communalist, linguistic and regionalistic outlooks are dividing the people and coming in the way of developing and unifying national and the international outlook.

Our educational aims stand in need of critical examination in the light of changing social, economic, political and cultural concerns.

Contribution of Schools:

One may expect schools to—

(*i*) kindle the moral and aesthetic sensibilities of children through exposure to appropriate objects, events and experiences.

(*ii*) help students understand and appreciate the values of democracy, secularism, scientific temper, social justice, national unity, etc.

(*iii*) enable students develop a concern for and commitment to these values.

(*iv*) enhance awareness of and sensitivity to moral aspects of major issues and concerns of modern life like poverty, illiteracy, human rights, environment, peace population.

(*v*) provide appropriate opportunities for students to practice and live by these values.

Education in Values—How?

Value education is not a one shot, unitary type of process. The following is to be done to educate the students in values—

(*i*) Awareness and understanding is to be built in the minds of students on aspects of democracy as right to freedom, responsibilities and duties, tolerance, respect for authority, accountability, etc.

(*ii*) Appropriate feelings and emotions of concern are to be aroused in the minds of students.

(*iii*) Attitudes of approval and feelings of appreciations are to be developed.

School and teachers will have their significant contribution towards value education if they have provided ample opportunities for children to be aware, to think and reflect, to question and criticize, to care and feel concern and to develop the disposition and will to act on one's convictions with reference to critical human concerns.

At last we can say that —

Mistake of the doctor is buried in the grave
Mistake of the engineer is cemented in the rocks,
but the mistake of the teacher is reflected to the nation.

Sir Aurobindo

REFERENCES

Peretra, J.D. Practical Moral Science, Grades 1-X, New Delhi; Neeta Prakashan, 1982.

Rohtdekar, S.R. et. al. (Ed.) Education in Human Values : Handbook for Teachers. Part II, Sri Sathya Sai Bal Vikas Education Trust, Prashanti Nilaya 1982.

Education in Human Values Series - Primer I and Primer II

Marni, T. Ramji - Value Oriented School Education, New Delhi, NCERT, 1973.

Vankataiah N. (Ed.) Value Education, New Delhi. APH Publishing Corporation, 1998.

16
Value based Education Ethos & Accountability in Teaching Profession

B.K. Savitri Bahen
L. Rawat

Life guided by spiritual wisdom leads a person on the path of right judgment and disciplined emotions. Spiritual wisdom is that art and science which is not learnt in Schools. It comes from one's sincere and meticulous practice of purity, goodness, virtue, serenity and above all Yoga Meditation. It is an art of living and science of good actions and culture of royalty and grace. It is a divine and most precious attainment of moral strength and self-control that leads the person to something higher than fulfilment so that one has no desires of short-gained temptations and guilt consciousness. The reasons for any deviant behaviour of some students is that they are not properly guided on the path of Spiritual Wisdom and Spiritually Happy Living.

Message of Nature

"Give me the courage to change things that I can change.
The patience to accept things that I cannot change
and the wisdom to know the difference"
So we need courage to adopt values and again 'Courage' is a value!

Essential Steps Towards Betterment of Education

- Formulating right policies.
- Spelling out right type of operational strategies
- Proper fixation of qualitative, quantitative, spatial, temporal, moral & social objectives.
- Proper prioritising of subjects
- Allocting sufficient resources
- Maintaining standards of courses/teachings at all levels.
- Properly organising finances, material & human resources.
- Ensuring inter-sectoral co-ordination
- Proper & effective monitoring
- Improving the system of examinations
- Efficient & well-oiled machinery of implementation, Followed by frequent reviews, keeping in mind the standards, inexorable imperatives & the changing situations.

VALUES AS AN ARROW

Trends in Institutions

Trends	*Values (necessary to keep up)*
• Commercialization	• Trusteeship
• Politicisation	• Self-control, accountability
• Sub-standard education	• Balance, precision
• Corruption	• Cleanliness (purity), honesty
• Strike	• Ahimsa, peace, Tolerance
• Renovation of curricula	• Pragmatism, courage to change

PRESSURES IN INSTITUTIONS

Pressures	Values (necessary to overcome)
• Vast Syllabus	• Industriousness, time-management
• Ill-equipped libraries, labs. & other facilities	• Precision, organizing, sense of responsibility
• Paucity of resources	• Dignity of profession
• Rote-learning, information imparting method	• Understanding, will to be enlightened
• Personal problems	• Harmony, self-esteem

Spiritual and value-based education - an urgent need of the hour!

VALUE EDUCATION

The word 'education' comes from the Greek word—Educe—which means to derive, to bring out. So, the very essential aim of education is to bring out the latent qualities, the goodness, to develop the inner potentialities of a child. So, a student can deal with adverse situations of life with positive qualities and courage. These positive qualities could be sincerity, truthfulness, innocence, love and non-violence, sympathy, co-operation, cleanliness of mind, body, heart, environment, good manners, sociability, self-control, respect for others, inner calmness, patience, enthusiasm and happy outlook, detachment, humility fearlessness and light nature, forgiveness, contentment, sattwic habits, respect for women, belief in the human dignity, creative mind, benevolence.

Meaning of the word 'value':

'Value' means the 'worth'. It is related to the life of human being. Developing values means making the human being a worthwhile person, so that everyone would like to associate with him.

Values lie at the heart of human behaviour. They motivate us and are the basis for our judgement. They determine how we live and in which direction we take our life. Values are what we share at every moment through our attitudes, behaviour and relationships. They are guiding principles.

There are values and virtues inherent in every human.

What education does is to reawaken and help to inculcate values in their everyday life.

How does value education help?

1. To eradicate negativism and develop a positive. attitude in thoughts, words and actions.
2. Develop self-esteem and respect towards society.
3. Helps the individual in contributing their skills and

energy towards creating a better society.

4. Develops strength.
5. Student's personality development.
6. Art of successful life.
7. Develops moral and human values.
8. Character building and Science of Behavioural transformation
9. Harmony and national integration
10. Improves your memory and concentration power
11. Creative activities on values.

Majority of the world's population today are largely influenced by material things. Thus creating cultures of accumulation, possessiveness, selfishness and ultimately greed. These ultimately stifle the inherent qualities of the human spirit, such as peace, love and respect. By implementing values into our lives we find that with genuine and respectful communication, an understanding among the people begins to take place.

LIVING VALUES: 12 CORE VALUES

The 12 core fundamental values are - co-operation, freedom, happiness, honesty, humility, love, respect, responsibility, simplicity, tolerance, unity and peace. Some group activities on each of these values with teaching methods of - reflection, visualisation, creativity, self-realisation, artistic work, etc. are being undertaken in their respective subjects.

Co-operation

The method to give co-operation is to use the energy of the mind to create vibrations of good wishes and pure feelings for the others and for the task. Courage, consideration, caring, and sharing provide a foundation from which co-operation as a process can be developed. It is possible only when there is a common goal and all members of society strive for it.

Freedom

Freedom implies the possibility for everyone to act and to express themselves as they wish without any constraints of external limitations. Full freedom functions only when rights are balance, with responsibilities and choice is balanced with conscience.

Happiness

Many people search for happiness through wealth, social status, good health or perfect relationships. Yet these are limited and temporary sources for happiness. The inability to hold onto pure and lasting happiness results from the absence of spiritual values and power. Happiness is the natural inheritance, which could be attained when our actions, attitudes, and attributes are pure and selfless.

Honesty

Honesty is when the inner-self is in harmony with the truth. It see everything as it is and not adding or subtracting from the whole. Honesty means there are no contradictions or discrepancies in thoughts, words, or actions.

Humility

Humility is the ability to listen and accept others. It enables one to become dependable, flexible, and adaptable. When one is humble, everyone 'bows down' to them, since everyone bows to those who themselves bow first.

Love

Love is a consciousness, which is simultaneously selfless and self-fulfilling. It flows from the truth that is wisdom. When love is combined with faith, it creates a strong foundation for initiative and action. Love is the catalyst for change.

Respect

To know one's own worth and to honour the worth of others is the true way to earn respect. Respect is an acknowledgement of the inherent worth and innate rights of both the individual and the collective.

Responsibility

A responsible person fulfils the assigned duty by staying

true to the aim. Duties are carried out with integrity and a sense of purpose. Responsibility in not a burden but an expression of care, which starts from the self. Responsibility towards the self creates a natural sense of responsibility of all facets of life.

Simplicity

Simplicity combines sweetness and wisdom in a sincere and natural way. In simplicity one is free from strenuous thinking and complications. Simplicity is the conscience which calls upon people to rethink their values.

Tolerance

Tolerance is peaceful co-existence. Tolerance is inner strength, which enables the individual to face and to transform misunderstandings and difficulties. While tolerance recognizes individuality and diversity, it removes masks and tension created by ignorance. The seed of tolerance is love, and love makes anything easier to tolerate.

Unity

Unity is harmony within and among individuals in the group. Unity is sustained by concentrating energy and focusing thoughts, by accepting and appreciating the value of the rich array of participants and the unique contribution each can make, and by remaining loyal not to one another but also to the task.

Peace

Peace is an inner state as well as an outer experience. Peace consists of pure thoughts, pure feelings, and pure vibrations. When the energy of thought, word, and action is balanced, stable, and free from any type of violence, the individual is at peace with the self, in relationships, and with the world.

To practise these values, practice of Rajyoga Meditation, i.e. connection and relation with the Supreme, soul empowers the oneself to implement these qualities in the life. Meditation improves inter-personal relationships.

ACTIVITIES ON VALUE-BASED EDUCATION BY BRAHMAKUMARIS

An Introduction

Prajapita Brahma Kumaris Ishwariya Vishva Vidyalaya (PBKIVV) is an educational institution which was founded in the year 1937 by the Supreme God Father Shiv Parmatma, & The Father of Humanity Prajapita Brahma Baba. The institution has now grown into a gigantic tree with more than 6000 branches, in India and in more then 80 countries. About 6 lakhs individuals daily study moral and spiritual values and practise meditation at these centres. The institution has gained global acceptance of its teachings and international recognition. Its International Headquarters is situated at Mt. Abu, (Raj). It is affiliated as an NGO to the Economic and Social Council (ECOSOC) of the UN and also to the UNICEF. It has been awarded a Peace Medal by the UN and also an international and five national 'Peace Messengers Awards' by the United Nations.

The Govt. of Mauritius has recognized it as an University by as Act of Parliament. The Govt. of Guyana has adopted the principle of starting the proceedings of their Parliament with 3 minutes Rajyoga Meditation. The Common Wealth of Russia has granted official recognition to this Spiritual Vishwa Vidyalaya in their country.

Mohanlal Sukhadia University of Udaipur (Raj.) has conferred the degree of Doctor of Literature (D.Litt) to Dadi Prakashmaniji, Chief of Brahmakumaris Institution.

EDUCATION WING

The institution has 'Academy for a Better World'-Gyan Sarovar, Mt. Abu. At this academic centre, under the 'Rajyoga Education & Research Foundation', several wings have been composed for the betterment of the Society, viz. education wing, medical, scientists and engineers, media, business-industries, women, political, social workers, jurists, administrators and executives, culture and art, rural wing. Through these wings value-based courses, and meditation experiences are given to different professional groups in their respective areas, which cater to their needs respectively.

Prominent Activities of Education Wing:

To create an awareness about value-based atmosphere in teaching profession various activities are undertaken. Values are related to consciousness. Thus, value-education is a 'conscious-training'. To impart such awareness in the following manner, programmes are being conducted:

- Every year conferences/seminars are organized on different themes for educationists at Mt. Abu, also at various other places.
- It hosts periodical Rajyoga Meditation Retreats/ Shivirs.
- It arranges teachers training courses on human, moral and spiritual values, viz., living values educational programme.
- It holds dialogues/workshops on current educational problems.
- It offers facilities for educational research on spirituality.
- It also publishes useful and relevant literature.
- It organizes lively value-based education fairs.
- It conducts, 'All India Children Personality Development Camps' at Mt. Abu.
- The Youth Wing organized several activities to guide students to live value-based life and to build up their positive personality and leadership qualities, so that they can face number of challenges in their life.
- Some of the youth activities so far conducted are—Bharat Ekta Yuva Pad Yatra, Akhil Bhartiya Naitik Jagruti Abhiyan, Sad Bhavna Yuva Cycle Yatra, Yuva Vikas Abhiyan, Positive Change Course, Youth Festivals, a number of essay, elocution, painting, drama, story/poem telling competition etc. were held on different virtues in India and abroad.
- Lectures were given in various departments of Delhi University-Geology, Zoology and in Delhi School of Economics.

- Lectures were given in Electronic Dept., at Govt.'s Engineering College, Kanpur and at various colleges of B'bay University, at Mysore University, and in some different states. The Mysore University has signed MoU with Brahma Kumaris Organisation to cater value-education to University students along with vocational/technical education, so that degree-holders can play very vital role in the society by using the knowledge of values in their life.
- PBKIVV has an institute at Yellapur in Karnataka where the Directorate of Education in Karnataka has officially been sending in-service teachers for courses in moral-orientation.
- PBKIVV runs Girls' Hostel at Indore (MP) and in Nadiad (Guj).
- Brahmakumaris' Youth wing has been awarded by the Gujrat Govt. for organizing national level youth activities on character building and positive personality development.
- All resource—persons of Education Dept. from Andhra Pradesh were sent on deputation to acquire training on application of 12 living values in school teachings.
- About 112 school teachers of BNSD Shiksha Niketan-Inter College, and 5 other schools of Kanpur (UP), together have acquired experiences through training on living values and its application in various subjects. For the new academic year 2003-04 they fixed the goal of attaining holistic personality development of students in their school. They also aim to develop quality of self discipline and freedom from exam-fear through meditation and exploring the values of respect, co-operation, responsibility, peace, love, etc. in their teaching methods.

Brahmakumaris' are sharing values for a better world. Such creative and successful workshops on value-based activities provide value experiences to the participants and bring transformation in their behaviour.

Universities all over India can apply these 12 wonder values in administration and introduce the practice of Rajyoga Meditation to overcome the problem of 'implementing paralysis'. Spiritual meditation evokes qualities of spiritual wisdom, self-control, emotional maturity and moral strength through which life is filled with joy and contentment.

17
Education & Human Values

Asha Sharma
S. P. Ahluwalia

The importance of providing education in human values to young ones has always been felt and emphasized by all great teachers, educationists and social reformers. But at the present juncture of the history of human civilization its importance has become extremely acute and critical dud to riotous interplay of diverse economic, technological, political, cultural and sociological factors causing as unprecedented moral decay and social disorganization. The greatest challenge before Indian education, therefore, is to inculcate in people a scientific temper, an unwavering commitment to the value of national integration equality, human dignity and universal brotherhood ignoring all barriers of caste, creed gender religion, language and region in the altogether different context from the classical past. The country's commitment to the provision this goal in a speedy fashion has to be seen in this complex milieu within which the educational system is currently functioning.

What are Human Values ?

"What are the values in Indian life which the citizens must preserve and build upon?" —The answer of the question would serve as the pointer to build our educational policies and practices in terms of various moral, social and spiritual values and in consonance with our cultural heritage and national aspirations. Righteousness, self-discipline, fellow-feeling, humanism, democratic sense and non-violence are some of the universally accepted and cherished value which need to be the nucleus of the new pattern of education to be so evolved.

Delving into the value-domain calls for a two-stage action. The first of these is to define what values are and to describe and differentiate between various value areas. The second to describe the process of value development. As defined by Kluckhohn (1957), "Value is a conception, explicit or implicit, distinctive of an individual or characteristic of a group, of the desirable which influences the selection from available modes, and ends of action".

Margenau (1959) defines - "Values" in terms of 'Satisfaction of human wants'. He says: "A value is the measure of 'satisfaction of human wants'. By the way Margenau says of two types of values: factual and normative. Factual values are observable in preferences, appraisals and desires of concrete people at a given time, and normative values are the ratings which people ought to give to value object. It is indicated that man work to satisfy their desires in the way which satisfy the desires of man is called value. The meaning of this saying is that the behaviour of man is motivated by the values.

Psychologically in the context of instructional objectives 'Valuing' falls under 'Affective Domain'. According to Krathwohl, et.al. (1964), "Affective Domain has five major categories—receiving (Attending), responding, valuing, organization and characterization by a value of value complex. The third category 'valuing' includes individual's commitment to a certain goal, idea or belief. The fourth category 'organization' indicates the level at which the learner builds up a value system that includes his behaviour. The last category in this taxonomy is 'characterization by value of value complex'. At this stage of development, the individual acts assiduously and consistently in accordance with the values he has internalized. Finally, he attains his beliefs, ideas and attitudes into a total philosophy or world view."

Value areas are differentiated according to the choice of

modes of actions adopted in attainment of the ultimate goals and ends. Borsodi (1965) stated, "Every human action is the reflection of an individual value, and every human institution, the outgrowth of a social value."

In philosophical context, "Values are those standards of a code for moral behaviour conditioned by one's cultural tenets and guarded by conscience according to which human being is supposed to conduct himself and shape his life pattern by integrating his beliefs, ideas and attitudes to realize cherished ideals and aims of life."

Rokeach (1973) defined value as an enduring belief, a specific mode of conduct or end state of existence along a continuum of relative importance. Any conception of human values if it is to be fruitful, it must be able to account for the enduring character of values as well as their changing character. The enduring character of values arises mainly by their initial teaching in learning in isolation from other values. A mode of behaviour or end state is always desirable.

In brief, human values are a sum total of several criteria operating in various spheres of life such as social relations, economy, politics, religion, cultural life and so on. Values are derived from history, tradition, religion, culture, education and aspiration of the future. They are subject to forces calling for renewals, adaptations and change.

All these are human values since they are all good things and they are concerned with the human society in some way of the other. Of course, as many of them as can be aimed at and made use of should be fostered by education. It is essential to concentrate on some specific and broad areas of values while launching any meaningful programme of education in human values.

Significance of Value-Oriented Education

It is unthinkable to have education without any kind of values. Value education means a positive effort for bringing about a synthesis of physical, intellectual, emotional, aesthetic, moral and spiritual values in a human being.

The success of education depends on how much balance it

brings about in an individual's personality by development of human values, so that he is happy, the society is civilised and the world is peaceful. The National Policy on Education (NPE 1986) has rightly emphasised the need for strengthening a system of value-oriented education. Such a value-based education would help in eliminating obscurantism, religious fanaticism, violence, superstition, fatalism, casteism, regionalism and such other parochial considerations. Value-oriented education has a profound positive content closely associated with our cultural heritage, national objectives and universal vision. It covers the entire process of learning and developing logical reasoning.

Several educationists in India and abroad have stressed the importance of promoting values through education , which is facing the crisis of character in different spheres of life. Radhakrishnan Commission (1949) held the view that in addition to the search for truth through scientific and scholarly pursuits an important task of education is a concern with values. Kothari Commission (1964-66) with its emphasis on education's role in national development includes among the functions of higher education cultivation of right interests, attitudes and moral and intellectual values. The national Policy on Education (1986) stated, "The growing concern over the erosion of essential values and an increasing cynicism in society has brought to focus the need for read-justments in the curriculum in order to make education a forceful tool for the cultivation of social and moral values."

Thus, value-based education inculcates in students a spirit of service, nationalism, patriotism, secularism, equality, democracy, scientific temper, etc., develops among them a sense of commitment to these values and provides them an opportunity to abide and live by these values. Hence, the main aim of value-based education is the evolution of a complete man, not just a social or biological entity. If education has relationship with the meaning of life, a proper value orientation of education becomes imperative.

Human Values: The Education Dimension

Amongst all the living, human life is the most evolved creation in the universe. The excellence or superiority of human life as compared to other living beings can be easily identified. Man is the only such unique creation in this universe who is under certain parameters free to make his own destiny. Now if man has to make his destiny, the question of values (life) comes up. Values are the quiding stars which provide a framework for his living. Each society formulates its own values and transmits them to its inhabitants. They may vary from one stage of the development of a particular society to anther . Therefore, what were considered to be essential in one stage of development may be equivalent in a different stage of development of that society.

Education, in broad general terms, can be looked upon as a social institution to promote a certain kind of life that is satisfying to individual in accordance with a preconceived pattern to individual in accordance with a preconceived pattern in corporating the cherished ideals and values of the society. In periods of crisis, it has to act as an agency of social control by fostering the basic values that hold the society together.

There are variety of agencies in the society which nurture the individual, which shape his thinking and inform his attitudes. Sociologists tell us that the most important among them are the family, the school and the society. To be precise these are the agencies which shape the character and conduct of the individual .

Whatever be the causes of the present situation, there is no need to labour the point that our society is passing through some sort of a crisis in values. The question here is whether this situation calls upon the school and teaching profession to assume any special role for value-education and if so what specific objectives can be laid down for the teaching profession in this area. Thus, teaching of desirable values should be the major concern of the system of Indian education.

Today, the question is: How to promote social consciousness or awareness in the Indian citizens? Which types of programmes should be arranged to acquaint the younger generations with India's ancient heritage, culture and emerging human values in the context of the new problems experienced by mankind. One of the ways to inculcate these values is by designing a course on human values and making it a part of the curriculum. It has to be stressed from the early stage of education so that it has a lasting effect on the future conduct and the way of life of the prospective adult. The objective of values-education should be development of an individual character-building which includes upholding of human dignity and self-respect. The main strategies for imparting values-education can be child-centred, teacher centred of experimental learning based. Appropriate educational approaches and systematic teaching strategies of value education spontaneously cultivate and inculcate human values in children who become citizens and conscious keepers of the nation later. The best way to transmit the values is "through practice rather than percepts, through example in action rather than more instructions" (Sharma, 1994). Prof, Kireet Joshi (1983) has rightly said:

"The secret of teaching values is to inspire and kindle the quest among the students by means of one's own example of character and mastery of knowledge. It is by embodying values within ourselves that we can really radiate values to our students."

Fine arts, music, creative writing, puppetry and theatre are to be given due place in the curricula right from school to the university level to promote and cultivate the feeling of community development, national integration, co-operation, independent judgement, faithfulness, neighbourhood and international understanding. The curriculum should, strike a balance between theory and practice. Creative work in fields of music, dance, literature, drama and visual arts is essential to cultivate the inherent tolerance of children. A variety of school programmes should be organised with care, enthusiasm and imagination, so that they prove effective in promotion of values among the pupils. Some of them which have rich potentialities are:

(*a*) Community prayer or prarthana Sabha

(*b*) Creative/productive teaching-learning situations,

(*c*) Sensitive training for democratic citizenship,
(*d*) Imaginative, cultural and recreational activities,
(*e*) Social/national service programme.

The value education must become an integral part of the entire education system. It should be taught as a compulsory subject upto the high school level. It should be made an examinable subject at the school level. Evaluation of value education should be based on compassion, self-reliance, respect and honesty. It has been rightly said that values are caught rather than taught. The right values are to be practised and demonstrated and not only preached.

To conclude, for value-orientation, it is relevant to fully utilize the life-setting and life-experience of students through a wide mix of pedagogic strategies wherein teacher occupies a position of key resource Teachers, therefore, should be aware of the important role they are called upon to play as professionals and citizens, as agents of development and change. They must make an effort to light a candle instead of cursing the darkness and sow the seeds of values education with a fond hope that they would diffuse their own fragrance towards the creation of a just and new society as they sprout and blossom.

REFERENCES

Bhat, R.K. 1996. Towards a value Based Education System, *University News*, Vol. XXXIV, No. 43, pp. 9-10.

Borosodi, R., 1965, The Neglected Science of Values. *Journal of Human Relations*, Vol. 13, No. 4, pp. 433-45.

Government of India, 1948-49. *Report of the University Education Commission*, New Delhi. Govt. of India.

Joshi, J.N., 1996. Empowering Teachers : Focus on value Education . *Journal of recent Researches in Education and Psychology*, Vol. 1, Nos. I-II, pp. 1-5.

Joshi, K., 1983. "An Outline Programme of Value Oriented Education and Relevant Dedagogical Suggestions". *"In Report of the working Group to Review Teachers' Training Programme"* (In the light of the need for value-orientation). New Delhi : Govt. of India. Ministry of Education and Culture, p. 39.

Kluckhohn, C., 1951. "Values and Value Orientations in the Theory of Action" In Talcott Parsons and Edward A. Shils et. al., *Toward A General Theory of Action*. Cambridge, Mass: Harvard University Press:

Krathwohl, D.R., Bloom B.S. And Masia, B.B, 1964 *Taxonomy of Educational Objectives : The Classification of Educational Goals, Handbook II : Affective domain*. New York: David Mckay Co.

Margenau, H. 1959. "The scientific Basis of Value Theory", in Maslow, A.H. (ed.), *New Knowledge in Human Values*. New York : Harper and Roe Publications.

Ministry of Education, 1964-66. *Report of the Education Commission*. New Delhi : Govt. of India.

Ministry of Human Resource Development, 1986 *National Policy On Education, 1986* Govt. of India New Delhi, Development of Education.

Passi, B.K. and Singh P. 1991. *Value Education*. Agra National Psychological Corporation.

Rani, S., 1996. Approaches to value Education and the role of the School and the curriculum. *University News*, Vol. XXXIV, No. 12, pp. 8-11.

Rokeach, M. 1973. *The Nature or Human Values*, London : Collier Mac Millan publications .

Ruhela. S.P., 1986. *Human Values and Education*. New Delhi : Sterling Pub.

Sharma, S.L. 1994 Role of Education in India's Development. *Academe* (marchi, Vol. IV, No. 1, pp. 17-20.)

18
Value Education—Challenges

Sapna Sharma

Values are described as the socially defined desires and goals that are internalised through the process of conditioning, learning and socialization. They are ideal to be sought. Values provide an understanding of better, precious. In other words, it can be said that values are 'preferences' an individual has towards objects, self, other, life, environment, etc. Value may be classified as:

Moral	Economic	Intellectual	
Values		Biological	Social
Aesthetic	Health	Political	Cultural

For development of an understanding of precious, preference, value education must aim at developing as awareness about values, provide experience through which children evolve their own value preferences. Value education is an attempt to ensure that children do not miss out on discerning those values that are compatible with social goals within political, economic and cultural context they live in.

Inculcation of values by individuals varies on as they grow and develop. For an infant, 'Value' is not necessarily a dimension of development. With age individual's experience broaden and with it his behaviours become varied to include subtle ones such values, that is during initial years one's main effort is to become familiar with the surroundings-recognise persons, objects and situations, to learn to respond, to seek, to share and to deal with. During this stage, foundations of social behaviour are built, mainly one's direct interactions with people and surroundings. Learning mainly is in the form of recognition, initiation and response. Most of these are concrete, immediate and short spanned. Through repetitive usage of these, the child acquires some socially acceptable behaviours as habits. Value development during this stage if all there is, gets restricted to habits-formation, recognition of do's and don'ts.

It is during the later childhood that the child begins to recognise that there are several 'goods' and 'bads', begins to understand the difference between the two and learns wish 'how one would want to be'. One also learns to discern things beyond one's self and immediate surroundings. No doubt, the child of this age (9-14 years) gets impressed by objects, persons and events quite easily and likes 'to become like...'. This tendency to like, desire, adopt and imitate is rather basic to learning values. This stage roughly coincides with the elementary stage of formal education system. It would be most appropriate to introduce focus on values in ways other than those already adopted for habit-formation during primary classes. In other words, the upper primary child can also learn values through understanding and appreciating certain facts and abstractions alongwith mechanical adherence.

Adolescence provides opportunity to an individual to articulate, to consolidate prior experience into a view point, guiding the present actions.

In other words, educating a child in values would pertain to making aware of these values, i.e. recognise, evolve and internalise, 'What to prefer', 'Which to prefer' in a given situation and be equipped for prioritising one's value structure in a given conflict situation. Effective instruction of inputs to achieve such an objective necessarily varied, indirect and suggestive. That is, value inculcation is a developmental instructional objective, which cannot be learnt in specific quantities but needs to be assimilated over time gradually education commission (1964-66) recommended that "Conscious and organised attempts he made for imparting education in social, moral and spiritual values with the help, whenever possible, of the ethical teaching of great religions".

Committee for Review of NPF (1986), set up in 1990 stated "Education must further provide a climate for nurture of values, both as personalised set of values forming one's character and including necessarily social, cultural and national values, so as to have a context and meaning for action and designs, and in order to enable the persons to act with conviction and commitment."

The committee (1976) also recommended that imparting of value education should be an integral part of entire educational process and school climate.

Various commissions and committees gave the significance of value education. For value development various educational programmes such as moral education, audio-visual educational programme or film or activity demonstration were organised by schools. Our formal educational system can provide a nurturing climate which helps individual discern positive aspiration and ideal on their own.

When the value education is so important for an individual personality development then what should be in our education process.

- In school there should be proper pattern of behaviour (relation between children, between Head & staff).
- Teacher occupies a pivotal role in imparting value education to the students. Does a teacher understand his student properly (Need, attitude, feeling, emotion).
- Education commission 1964-66 stated that "every teacher whatever the subject he teaches must necessarily does ensure that in teaching of his subject and in his dealing with his pupils, fundamental values such as integrity and social responsibility are brought out."
- Does curriculum provide enough opportunity for pupil to acquire an amount of Kn. that is essential for morally responsible living in our democratic society.
- Does different subjects learning help the student understand the Kn. of these subjects to identify the

value in it and internalise these.

- Attitude to materialistic life and complex modern society is effecting the value education.
- School assembly, curricular and to curricular activities celebration of festivals, work experience, teem games, sports, subjects clubs, social service programmes all these can help in inculcating the value of cooperation and mutual regard, honesty and integrity, discipline and social responsibility.

If we get the answers of above questions, we can say that value education can develop the values in individual behaviour.

For this school should provide a healthy climate for sharing responsibility, community life and relationship.

All teachers should be regarded as teachers of value education. All subjects can be used for inculcation if right value. So value education should prepare individual for participation in social life and acceptance of the same.

REFERENCES

1. Ministry of Education, 'Report of Secondary Education Commission 1952-53', Government of India, New Delhi.
2. Ministry of Education, 'Report of Education Commission 1964-66, Government of India, New Delhi.'
3. Ministry of Human Resource Development, National Policy on Education 1986 & Programme of Action, Government of India, New Delhi.
4. MHRD, Report of Committee for Review of National Policy on Education, 1986, Government of India, New Delhi. 1990.
5. Gupta, N.L. Human Value in Education, Concept Publishing Company, New Delhi-2000.
6. Sharma, Y.K., Foundations in Sociology of Education, Kaniska Publishers, New Delhi-2001.
7. 'Value' is not necessarily a dimension of development. With age individual's experience broadens and with it his behaviours become varied to include.

19
Value-Oriented Education for Growth and Development: An Appraisal

Sapna Verma
Payal Khanna

India is passing through a very critical phase of her history where long cherished values such as respect for all religions, righteous conduct, abstinence from alcoholic drinks and drugs are undergoing fast erosion. Since Indian society comprises of multi-linguistic, multi-racial and multi- religious groups, it is quite important to impart value-oriented education to the learners at different levels of education. Value-oriented education has the unique capacity to transform a diseased mind into a very young, fresh, innocent, healthy, natural and active mind. Value-oriented education means inculcating in the children a sense of humanism, deep concern for the well being of others and the nation. Knowledge of human values will lead them to an awareness of self and others, thus making their interactions and responses more than fruitful. Though much has been spoken and written about education in values, it has not been translated into action on a large scale basis covering all students belonging to different socio-economic strata. There is need for a systematic and concrete action in this respect.

The Indian society is heterogeneous and consists of several strata. The social background of the family can exert a powerful influence on the developing personality of a young person. The values are different in upper, middle and lower class children.

Investigators have found that differences in the social background are related to significant and crucial differences among individuals. Compliance of parental values is observed in low social background (Tuma & Norman, 1991). The life values of children belonging to low socio-economic-status are affected by parental ambitions who expect them to behave as adults. Long before their age due to economic crises (Bossard, 1948; Davis, 1941). Children belonging to low SES deny various privileges and enriching experiences enjoyed by upper and middle class children. In short there is ***no child's world*** in lower class.

In India, where the population has crossed over one hundred crores, more than fifty percent of the population is living below poverty line. Therefore, it is quite necessary to impart value- oriented education to the children who belong to low SES. One of the ways to inculcate these values is by designing a course on human values and making it a part of the curriculum. It has to be stressed from the early stages of education so that it has a lasting effect on the future conduct and the way of life to the prospective adult. The main strategies of value education should be child- centered, teacher-centered and experimental learning strategies. Appropriate educational approaches and systematic teaching strategies of value educational approaches and systematic teaching strategies of value education spontaneously cultivate and inculcate human values in children who will become citizens and conscious keepers of the nation later. The best way to transmit the value is "through practice rather than percepts, through example in action rather than more instructions," (Sharma 1994). Joshi (1983) has rightly said, "The secret of teaching values is to inspire and kindle the quest among the students by means of one's own example of character and mastery of knowledge. It is by embodying values within ourselves that we can radiate values to our students."

Fine Arts, music, creative writing, poetry and theatre are to be given due place in the curricula right from school to the university level to promote and cultivate the feeling of community, development, national integration, cooperation, independent judgement, faithfulness, neighbourhood and international understanding. A variety of school programme should be organised with care, enthusiasm and imagination, so that they prove effective in promotion of values among the pupils.

In this way value-oriented education must become an integral part of the whole educational system. It should be taught as a compulsory subject upto the high school level, so that it has a lasting effect on ***going to be adult generation*** for their full growth and development.

REFERENCES

Bossard, J.H.S. (1948). The Sociology of Child Development, New York : Harper.

Davis, M.R. (1941). Social Status and the Moral Development of the child. British Journal of Educational Psychology, 1, 75-95.

Joshi, K. (1983) An outline programme of value-oriented education and relevant pedagogical suggestions. In report of the working group to review teachers' training programme (In the light of the need for value orientation). New Delhi : Govt. of India, Ministry of Education and Culture, 39.

Muralidharan, K. (2002) Values in Education in India's Development. Academe (March), 4 (1), 17-20.

Sinha, S.N.P. (2001) Towards Inculcating Values in Education. University News, 39(43), 1-3.

Tuma, E-& Norman, L. (1991) Family S.E & Adolescent Attitudes to Authority. University of Florida, by Regional Office Scott. Foresman & Company, USA, 65.

20
Value Education: A Psychological Point of View

Anurag Bhatnagar

The process of modernisation is in progress. It is not bad because it is a healthy attitude to life to be aware of scientific and technological means which are giving every comfort to human beings and are trying to ameliorate its sufferings. But, modernisation without moral development is indeed a curse. Prof. Lon Whit warned, "To-day technology has become so terrible that God alone can save the world. There is a need for creating a balance between modernisation and moral values." It is thus that National Policy on Education - 1986 declared (p. 21, Para 8:4) "The growing concern over the erosion of essential values and an increasing cynicism in society has brought to focus the need for readjustment in the carriculum in order to make education a forceful tool for the cultivation of social and moral values". The same was emphasized by the Education commission (1964-66). The commission said, "It has become necessary and urgent to adopt active measures to give a value-orientation to education." (p. 19). It observed, "modernisation does not mean-least of all in our national situation—a refusal to recognise the importance of or to inculcate necessary moral spiritual values and self-discipline". Importance of value education has been very much emphasized by Kireet Joshi (1983), ex-education advisor to Government of India who wrote profusely on the need for value education. Norman C. Dowsett (1977) Sri Aurobindo's follower also stressed the need for value education. He said, "education must be founded upon spiritual values." It is not only in our country that value based education is prized so much. Value education has been stressed by educationists in several other countries too.

John Deway (1939) in America wrote, "A culture which permits science to destroy traditional values but which distrusts its power to create new ones is a culture which is destroying itself." He had a strong conviction that primary justification for school education was its role in strengthening the ethical values. In 1895 Dewey had written that, "the ultimate problem of all education is to co-ordinate the psychological and social factors." By social factors we mean social values.

Thus, the importance of value education is universally recognized. There cannot be any controversy about this. But, the crux of the whole problem is how to achieve this goal. Efforts are no doubt being made. At the national level the NCERT has recently augmented their efforts by establishing a separate cell to promote values. They have started publishing a quarterly journal on value education, have built a moderately good library of publications on value education, have conducted researches on value education. Yet, a greal confusion persists as to what is value education, what should be the objective of teaching values, how values can be taught.

Psychological Point of View:

Analyzing from psychological point of view it appears to me that value education has its two levels of stages : one, the awareness of the value; and second, its incorporation in the actual behaviour, i.e. living the value. At the moment the efforts being made are, by and large, confined to the awareness level only. But awareness does not guarantee that actual behaviour of the individual who is aware of a value will also be value-oriented. And if values learned remain confined only to the awareness level, they are of no use from social point of view. Hence, value education or learning of values to my mind should mean changing or shaping human behaviour as implied in the respective value. To be practical, therefore, development of behavioural component of values should be the objective of value education. This, however, should not mean that consciousness or awareness component should be disregarded. This is also unavoidable as, psychologically even for the development of behavioural aspect of value its awareness is essential. But, to be realistic, value learned should mean value lived. Simply knowing that telling the truth is good and that nobody should tell a lie is of no avail. This is hypocrisy. This does no good to anybody.

The concept of behavioural value emphasizes that people should learn and behave as implied in the learned value. If truth- speaking is a value its learning will be complete when the person, by and large, speaks the truth. This level of value education, if not impossible, is difficult enough. That is why it is said that, "values are caught, not taught." Psychologically speaking it amounts to changing the man. To change the man is difficult but not impossible. Man changes even if he does not want. This is, psychologically, a fact. But, to change the man in a planned way as implied in a particular value is very difficult but not impossible. This too is a psychological fact.

Strategy of Value Development:

Psychologically, every socially desirable behaviour is a value. Or we can say every value is a desirable behaviour. If it is a behaviour it can be analysed psychologically. It can be controlled and directed in the value-oriented direction. There are two strategies which may help us Skinner's operant conditioning theory of learning and Bandura's imitative or modelling technique. Skinner's theory in the simplest language says 'reward the value-oriented desirable behaviour and ignore or punish its anti-behaviour. Albert Bondura, a psychologist, has shown that people learn desirable and undesirable behaviours by imitating models around them. All people learn desirable as well as undesirable behaviours only in this way. If the society rewards undesirable behaviour, people learn undesirable behaviours. If, on the other hand, society rewards good ethical behaviours the people learn desirable behaviours. The process of imitation also proves the same. If it is found repeatedly and consistently that in a society corrupt behaviours push the people up and good behaviours go unnoticed then more and more people are templated to imitate the corrupt. If it is otherwise, people learn to shape themselves well and in desirable ways. If the model is highly effective just one single person in the society can bring about a big change in the masses. Mahatma Gandhi may be considered one such an effective model. Currently, there is utter lock of such models in our society. So there is the value crisis. The current strategies that are being adopted at institutional levels will not bring any fruitful result. I am quite skeptic about this kind of approach to value education. It is not in conformity with the principles of psychology. In our society the man who says at the top of his voice, 'never tell a lie, tells hundred times more lies'. In the midst of such models whose number is growing by leaps and bounds. How can values be learned by people? I leave this question for you to think and decide.

Thank you very much.

REFERENCES

Bandura, Albert : *Principles of Behaviour Modification,* New York, Holt, Rinehart and Winston, Inc., 1969.

Dewey, John : *Freedom and Culture,* New York, G.P. Putnam's Sons. 1939, P. 154.

Joshi, Kireet , "Can Values Be Taught", *Report of the Working Group to Review Teachers' Training Programmes.* Ministry of Education and Culture, Government of India, 1983.

Ministry of Human Resource Department, Govt. of India, Deptt. Of Education, New Delhi, *National Policy on Education, 1986,* p. 21.

Ministry of Education, Govt. of India, *Report of the Education Commission,* (1964-66), p. 19.

Swami Ranganathananda : *Eternal Values for a Changing Society* Vol. IX 1986, Bhartiya Vidya Bhavan, Bombay.

21
Aurobindo's Educational Philosophy: A Matrix of Integral Education

Gurpreet Kaur
H.S. Randhawa

Sri Aurobindo has a unique concept of education beneficial to both educand and the society. He wanted to have national system of education, which "must be up to date in form and substance and modern in life and spirit."[1] He conceived a true and living education that took into account the man, the individual in his commonness and his uniqueness, the nation or the people and universal humanity.

He was not ready to accept anything on that pretext that it was a part of India's rich past because he feels, "We cannot be satisfied with a mere resuscitation of some past principle, method and system that may have happened to prevail at one time in India, however great it was or in consonance with our past civilization and culture."[2] Similarly he rejected the argument of blindly following our educational system on the pattern of European civilization because he knew that "Europe built up her ancient culture on a foundation largely taken from the East, from Egypt, Chaldea, Phoenicia, India.. ... The scientific, rationalistic, industrial pseudo-domestic civilization of the West is now in process of dissolution and it would be a lunatic absurdity for us at this moment to build blindly on that sinking foundation."[3] According to Sri Aurobindo, each individual and community should have a system of education suitable to its genius. This is necessary both for the perfect working of society and individual. Here Sri Aurobindo reiterates what ancient Greek and Indian philosophers of education had already emphasized. According to Plato, "each social element should do that which it is most fitted to do, thus contributing to the common stock, the best that it has to give and receiving from each other element that of which it is itself most in need."[4]

The main aim of education according to him is the physical development and physical purity of the child because it is the body, which performs all religious ceremonies. He is of the opinion that physical development and purification are the two pillars on which the edifice of spiritual development can be built.

The guiding principle of Sri Aurobindo's educational philosophy was the awakening of the individual as a spiritual being. It should be related to life, truth and self-mastery of the child. For him, education is a process of transforming man into an integral man. Writing about the nature of such a transformation, Aurobindo observed "There will be needed a change of the habitual and normal nature of man as he is new to a supreme and divine spiritual nature. There will be needed in a word a yoga which shall be at once a yoga of integral will and its works, a yoga of integral love, adoration and devotion and a yoga of an integral spiritual perfection of the whole being and of all its parts and states and powers and motions."[5]

Integrality of education is thought as a process of organic growth, and the way in which various faculties could be developed and integrated. It takes care of each child's inclination, rhythm of progression and law of development, Swabhava (inherent disposition) and Swadharma (inner culture). Integral education is not considered as a blend of a number of subjects and even mixture of varieties of faculties. The idea is to provide facilities for varieties of faculties, varieties of subjects and various combinations of pursuits of knowledge.

In brief, his integral education has two functions to perform (a) it gives an integral view of the universe to the pupil. A student of science should also look at life, society and the universe around not only from a scientific perspective but also from those of humanities, fine arts and the social sciences. This function of education has also been highlighted by the University Education Commission of 1948 chaired by Dr. S. Radhakrishnan (b) Education must attempt at an all-round balanced, harmonious and integrated development of the individual in place of piecemeal, isolated and pigeonholed one. The physical, social and emotional, intellectual and spiritual life and powers of the child should be tapped and unfolded in an integrated way. This will lead to the proper development of the nation.

He believed that with the increase of integral men in the society, evil will decrease and freedom, equality, justice, brotherhood, knowledge, peace and live will replace slavery, untouchability, ignorance, exploitation, prejudices, vanity, jealousies and hatred. His integral society consists of human beings in physical form radiating the virtues of a superman. He has very high expectations from the education about the benefits that will be gained by the children. He observed, "They should be children of the past, possessors of the present, creators of the future. The past is our foundation, the present our material, the future our aim and summit."[6]

In the opinion of Sri Aurobindo, the main aim of education was 'self-realisation'. In one of his writings, he has highlighted the aim of education thus, "education will at no time, lose sight of man's highest object, the awakening and development of his spiritual being."[7] At another place he has observed, "the chief aim of education should be to help the growing soul to draw out that in itself which is best and make it perfect for a noble use."[8]

His concept of self-realisation is based on the teaching of the Upanishads. (The Taithiriya Upanishad has described the self as surrounded by five layers constituted by five sheaths) the panchakosas. When Aurobindo speaks of an education of the self, he means an education relating to all these five layers. By this combined form only, the education becomes an integral one. The outline of his education can be presented in the following form:

Cells/Layers	*English Translation*	*Appropriate Education*
Annamaya Kosha	Physical Cell	Physical Education
Pranamaya Kosha	Vitality Cell	Vital Education (of sense organs)
Manamay Kosha	Mental Cell	Intellectual Education
Vijanamaya Kosha	Psychic Cell	Social and Emotional Education
Anadamaya Kosha	Spiritual Cell	Spiritual or Supramental Education

According to Sri Aurobindo, education is a progressive, interrelated coordinated and meaningful activity for the stimulation and growth of all these cells. Aurobindo explains his concept of Integral education in these words, "Education to be complete must have principal aspects relating to the five primary activities of the human being: the physical, the vital, the mental, the psyche and the spiritual. Usually these phases of education succeed each other in a chronological order following the growth of the individual. This however does not mean that one should replace another but that all must continue, completing each other, till the end of life."[9]

The aim of education according to ancient Indian thinkers was described as Chitta-Vratti-Nirodh. Thus chitta is the instrument of education. Education is a process of the control of mind so that realization of the true self may be brought about in the mind. Sri Aurobindo postulates mind or antahkharana as the instrument of education. The first line of Karma Yogin published in Feb-March 1910 was, "The true basis of education is education is the study of the human mind – infant, adolescent, and adult."[10] Mind or Antahkharana, according to Sri Aurobindo, consists of the following four layers:

(a) **Chitta**: This is the reservoir of past memories and mental impressions. It must be distinguished from the specific act of memory. It is the foundation on which all the other layers stand. This has two aspects – passive and active memory respectively. The passive memory or chitta needs no training; it is automatic and naturally sufficient to its task. There is not the slightest object of knowledge coming within its field, which is not secured, placed and faultlessly preserved in that admirable receptacle. It is the active memory, a higher but less perfectly developed function, which requires education and training.

(b) **Manas or Mind Power**: This sixth sense receives images of things through sensation of different sense organs like sight, sound, smell, taste and touch. It also directly receives mental images and forms mental impressions. These sensations and impressions supply raw material to thought. Thus the training of sense organs and organs of activity is a prelude to all sound thinking and the first step in a proper education. Prof. Raina says, "The hand, for instance, should be trained to reproduce what the eye sees and the mind senses. The speech would be trained to a perfect expression of the knowledge which the whole antahkharana possesses."[11]

(c) **Intellect or Buddhi**: The third layer is the true instrument of thought. It provides shape and order to the knowledge attained by the other parts of the machine. The intellectual is an organ composed of parts of functions divisible into two important classes, — the functions and faculties of the right hand and the functions and faculties of the left hand. The faculties of the right hand are comprehensive, creative and synthetic while the faculties of the left hand are critical and analytic. In other words, judgement, imagination, memory and observation belong to the right hand and comparison and reasoning belong to the left hand. In the words of Sri Aurobindo, "The critical faculties distinguish, compare, classify, generalize, deduce, infer and conclude. They are the component parts of the logical reason. The right hand faculties comprehend, command, judge, in their own right, grasp, hold and manipulate. The right hand mind is the master of the knowledge, the left hand its servant. The left hand touches only the body of language; the right hand penetrates its soul."[12] Both these types of abilities are essential for the working of human reason. So according to Aurobindo, both require training and development in a sound system of education.

(d) **Supra-normal faculties**: Here Sri Aurobindo defines faculties as abilities. These super normal faculties consist of the functions included in the working of psi phenomena such as ESP (Extra-Sensory perception) including telepathy and clairvoyance and PK (Psycho-Kinesis) and the phenomena of genius. These according to Sri Aurobindo cannot be developed by instruction. The educator can only remove the impediments in their growth. He should see that these faculties might develop properly without any hindrance. It is to be noted here that Sri Aurobindo has not only stressed to significance of these supra-normal faculties, but he has also given suggestions for their control in his yogic writings. For Sri Aurobindo, as per Aldous Huxley, "a perfect education is one which trains up every human being to fit into the place he or she is to occupy in the social hierarchy, but without in the process destroying his or her individuality."[13]

Thus the main aim of education according to Sri Aurobindo is not only to acquire information but also to develop mind, reasoning, inner strength, spirituality, morality, body and artistic skill. Indra Sen aptly writes, "The aim and principle of a true natural education is not certainly to ignore modern truth and knowledge but to take our foundation on our own being, our own mind, our own spirit'[14]

In the sphere of curriculum, Aurobindo suggested integrated curriculum for the all-round development of the personality of the child. Science and Humanities both were given preference. He said, "It is true that certain subjects are more apt to develop faculties than others; the power of accurate reasoning is powerfully assisted by Geometry, Logic and Political Economy; one of the most important results of language is to refine and train the power of comparison and differentiation than an intelligent study of history. There is in fact hardly any subject, the sciences of calculation excepted, which in the hands of a capable teacher does not give room for the development of all the general faculties of the mind."[15] Sri Aurobindo gave importance only to those subjects, which may be helpful in the physical, mental, moral, social, vital and spiritual progress of the child. He was not in favour of that syllabus, the weight of which may hamper the onward progress of the students.

Here his curriculum is analysed through the ambit of his general philosophy. The metaphysics of Sri Aurobindo suggested the study of literature and social sciences. His epistemology suggested integral education that was correlation of different subjects. His axiology stressed on moral and spiritual training and common aspects of religion i.e. universal brotherhood. His aesthetics suggests painting, poetry, music, photography and other creative activities. His logic stressed the training of logical faculties, mental activities and freedom in expression.

As described earlier, his integral education consists of five aspects of education physical, vital, mental, psychic and spiritual or supramental education. According the scholar describes the syllabus mentioned under each fold of education–

(1) **Physical Education**: A healthy body is a mirror of the personality of man. Sri Aurobindo has described physical education as the basic pillar of education. He brought daily exercise, sports, and discussion on different organs of human body, hygiene rules, nutrition, clean food and healthy environment like topics under educational syllabus for keeping human body healthy. Aurobindo says, "Body building is nation building. Children's health is wealth for the country."[16]

Again he adds, "A development of the physical consciousness must always be a considerable part of our aim, but for that the right development of the body itself is an essential element. Health, strength and fitness are first needs, but the physical frame itself must be the best possible. A life divine in the material world implies necessarily a union of two ends of existence, the spiritual summit and the material base. The soul with the basis of its life established in matter ascends to the heights of the spirit but does not cast away its base, it joins the heights and the depths together."[18] In the Ashram physical fitness was given predominant importance and children were dissuaded from taking recourse to physical debility as an alibi for shirking one's responsibility.

It was emphasized by Sri Aurobindo that real beauty lies in one's good physique and so efforts must be made to maintain body free from diseases. The Mother added, "I have said that from a young age children should be taught to respect good health, physical strength and balance. The great importance of beauty must also be emphasized. A young child should aspire for beauty, not for the sake of pleasing others or winning their admiration, but for the love of beauty itself; for beauty is the ideal which all-physical life must realize. Every human being has the possibility of establishing harmony among the different parts of his body and in the various movements of the body in action. Every human body that undergoes a rational method of culture from the beginning of its existence can realize its own harmony and thus become fit to manifest beauty. When we speak of the other aspect of an integral education, we shall see what inner conditions are to be fulfilled so that this beauty can one day be manifested."[19]

(2) **Vital Education**: The second important step of his educational ladder is vital education. He says, "Vitality means life force-whereas there is life in plant or animal or man there is life – force. Without the vital there can be no life in matter and no living action. The vital is a necessary force and nothing can be done or created in the bodily existence, if the vital is not there as an instrument."[20] He brought arts, music, drama, dance, and drawing and painting under it. Besides he has favoured the need of a moral education in any sound system of education. This moral training, according to him, can be imparted by suggestion and not by command. "The wildness and recklessness of many young natures are only the overflowing of an excessive strength, greatness and nobility. They should be purified, not discouraged."[21] Again Sri

Aurobindo says, "The vital has not be killed or destroyed but purified and transformed by the psychic and spiritual control."[22]

He has divided the vital into four forms (a) mental vital (b) emotional vital (c) central vital (d) lower vital.

(a) *Mental Vital*: Its area extends from throat to heart. Sri Aurobindo says, "The mental vital which gives a mental expression by thought, speech or otherwise, to the emotions, desires, passions, sensations and other movements of the vital beings."[23]

(b) *Emotional Vital*: It is related with the anterior side of the heart. The posterior portion of the heart is connected with the Chaitya Purusha. Sri Aurobindo says, "The emotional vital is the seat of various feelings such as love, joy, sorrow, hatred and the rest."[24]

(c) *Central Vital*: Its area extends from heart to navel. Sri Aurobindo says, "The central vital is the seat of the stronger vital longings and reactions e.g. ambition, pride, fear, love of fame, attractions and repulsions, desires and passion of various kinds and the field of many vital energy."[25]

(d) *Lower Vital*: It is related with the lower portion of the navel. Sri Aurobindo says, "Lower vital which is occupied with small desires and feelings such as make the greater part of daily life. e.g. food desires, sexual desires, special likings, dis-likings, vanity, quarrels, love, praise, anger and little wishes of all kinds."[26]

So in the opinion of Sri Aurobindo, educational curriculum should encompass all aspects, which may ennoble all constituents of the vital. The Mother said, "this vital education has two principal aspects, very different in their aims and methods, but both equally important. The first concerns the development and use of the sense organs. The second is progressing awareness and control of the character, culminating in its transformation."[27]

(3) **Mental Education**: Mental Education has a very

significant role in the educational system of Aurobindo. He brought only those topics under educational syllabus that widens the mental horizon of the children. He accepted the importance of the following subjects for augmenting the mental faculties of the child:

(A) *Mother tongue*: Sri Aurobindo wants to introduce first of all, child's mother tongue for his complete mental development. It is only after the mastery of one's own mother tongue that one can hope to learn other languages. A mastery of the mother tongue will open to the educand treasures of literature and history of his own country. This is very much in agreement with Gandhi's scheme of basic education.

(B) *Hindi, English, Sanskrit*: Sri Aurobindo has considered Sanskrit to be very important subject. According to him the teaching of Sanskrit should be started from the first class for introducing Indian culture to the child. He wanted that the teaching of Hindi and English should begin from third and fourth class respectively. The Mother said, "Hindi is good only for those who belong to a Hindi speaking province. Sanskrit is good for all Indians."[28] And she added, "The Sanskrit ought to be the national language of India."[29]

(C) *History and Geography:* According to Sri Aurobindo, the study of geography and history is essential for knowing about environment and archaeology respectively. The mother said, "History and Geography can only become interesting to minds that are eager to know the earth on which they live."[30]

(D) *Science*: Sri Aurobindo is of the opinion that by learning science through environmental techniques, the interest of the students can be developed in it. According to the Mother, "The sciences, if you study them deep enough, will teach you the unreality of the appearances and thus lead you to the spiritual reality."[31]

(E) *Mathematics*: Sri Aurobindo has given pre-eminence to mathematics for mental development and day-to-day working of our life. The Mother said, "As per Arithmetic, I am much more in favour of practical than of written arithmetic, with an emphasis on the development of the faculty of mental arithmetic. It is more difficult but it greatly increases the capacity for inner visualization and reasoning. It is very effective way of developing true intelligence instead of memorized knowledge."[32]

(4) **Spiritual or Supramental Education**: Sri Aurobindo considers the realization of spirituality as the prime motive of human life. So he wants that proper arrangement must be made in the educational process for the acquisition of spiritual values. This does not imply the extinction of the individual but his enrichment through contact with the Absolute. The idea for psychic and spiritual education is based upon three points: (a) education should impart to the human being a steady exploration of a thing that is inmost in the psychological complexity of human consciousness, (b) by developing psychic and spiritual faculties of knowledge, the psychic and spiritual domain of human life are explored, (c) by developing psychic and spiritual consciousness, the disbalance between the matter and the spirit can be bridged. Sri Aurobindo has drawn a distinction between psychic and spiritual in these words: In psychic life the individual senses an unbroken continuity in the world of forms and observes level as an immortal function in endless time and limitless space. The spiritual consciousness goes beyond time and space and is integrated with infinite and the eternal. Prof. Raina aptly observes, "Aurobindo says that in psychic life selfishness must be discarded, but in the spiritual life there is no sense of the separate self. He insists that it is not annihilation of the individual but its transformation, which is the end of integral education. When man attains such education there is total transformation of matter. He calls it supramental education as it will work, not only upon the consciousness of individual beings but upon the very substance

of which they are built and even upon the physical environment in which they live."[33] At present International Centre of Education at Pondicherry is the living example of spiritual education. Dr. Sunil Behari Mohanty writes, "Spiritual education is provided at the centre in an informal way. According to the ideal, it is provided by making children stay in spiritual atmosphere of the ashram and by the example practice that. No one is instructed to follow certain rites or rituals."[34] The Mother and Sri Aurobindo have not fixed any definite curriculum for spiritual and supramental education. As for spiritual development, the Mother once said, that "this cannot be done by any external method, therefore there are no prescribed courses or observances."[35]

To sum up, this process of all-round development through education is compared in the Upanishads to charioteer. The chariot is being compared to the body, the horses to the senses, the rope to the mind, the intellect to the force applied to the body and charioteer to the spirit. For reaching the destination i.e. self-realization, charioteer should control the horses by exerting proper force on the rope. In other words, that person is a realized soul whose cognitive, affective and psychomotor domains have developed to the full.

REFERENCES

1. Sri Aurobindo, *A Preface on National Education*, Pondicherry, Aurobindo Press, p. 4.
2. *Ibid.*, p. 2.
3. *Ibid.*, p. 6.
4. Quoted by R.K. Nettleship in *The Theory of Education*, 1935, p. 4.
5. Sri Aurobindo, *Essays on the Gita*, Calcutta; Arya Publishing House, p. 557.
6. Sri Aurobindo, *On Education*, Pondicherry: Aurobindo Press, p. 12.
7. Sri Aurobindo, *Arya* (1920-21), A Preface on National Education.
8. Sri Aurobindo, *A System of National Education*, Calcutta, Arya Publishing House.
9. The Mother, *On Education*, pp. 96-97.
10. *Ibid.*, p. 99.

11. Raina, M.K., Sri Aurobindo, *Prospects,* 2000, p. 61.
12. Sri Aurobindo. *On Education,* Pondicherry, Aurobindo Ashram, 1990, p. 24.
13. Huxley, A., *A Proper Studies,* London: Chatto and Hindus, 1928, p. 136.
14. Sen, Indra, *Integral Education,* Pondicherry, Aurobindo Ashram, p. 4.
15. Sri Aurobindo, *A New Education for a New Consciousness,* All India Magazine, Oct. 1990, Sri Aurobindo Society, p. 4.
16. Quoted by Narayan Prasad in *Education for New Life,* p. 45.
17. Sri Aurobindo, *The Supramental Manifestation Upon Earth,* p. 17.
18. *Bulletin,* April, 1951.
19. Sri Aurobindo, *Letters on Yoga,* Part I, *op. cit,* p. 346.
20. Sri Aurobindo, *A System of National Education,* p. 20.
21. Aurobindo, *Letters on Yoga,* Part I, *op. cit.,* p. 346.
22. *Ibid.,* p. 334.
23. *Ibid.,* p. 334
24. *Ibid.,* p. 334
25. *Ibid.,* p. 335
26. *Bulletin,* August, 1951.
27. The Mother, *On Education,* p. 219.
28. *Ibid.,* p. 219.
29. *Ibid.,* p. 235.
30. The Mother, *Light for Students,* Pondicherry, Aurobindo Ashram, 1971, p. 40.
31. The Mother, *On Education, op. cit.* p. 236.
32. Raina, M.K., Sri Aurobindo, *Prospects,* p. 67.
33. Mohanty, Sunil Behari, *Theory and Practical of Integral Education,* Pondicherry, Navjyoti Karyalaya, Aurobindo Ashram, 1985, p. 88.
34. The Mother, *On Education,* Part 2, Advice to Students and Teachers, Pondicherry, Sri Aurobindo Ashram, 1990, p. 5.
35. Aurobindo, *A System of National Education, op. cit,* p. 20.

22
Education in Values

Vijaishri Bhati

A better life for Man is possible and it is contingent on *man* himself. This has been the core of the philosophies right through the ages, although, they had much to differ as to the structure of the world, nature of reality, nature of knowledge of the concept of knowledge and the concept of values. Both collectivists like Karl Marx and others and individualists like Nunn?, Spencer and others, have put their faith in the possibility, rather inevitability of human betterment. The history of Educational Thought is the testimony of the fact that the perfection of man has been the focal point and all educational efforts accorded with this fact. Education has always aimed at the development of the human personality. Of course, the weightage on any one aspect or certain qualities have been shifting in different periods in all the societies. But it has always been the chief concern of education to inculcate the qualities of *head, hand* and *heart*. Whenever there has been a lack of integration in these aspects of personality, need has risen to reform education criterion to evaluate the integrated personality also are subject to shift in emphasis either on individual or social aspect. Thus, ends of education are constantly questioned and reforms are effected accordingly. Such questions were quite prominent in the history of Indian Education. In recent times too, it is realised that there is need to give rethinking to the total effect of education on the development of personality, where it comes to mean, besides the qualities of *head* and *hand*, the qualities of *heart*.

The life pattern in the societies, with special reference to ours, is undergoing a change. It is a must in the wake of scientific and technological advances that a new culture get place and influence our social life. The flux and influx is the constant phenomena. At the time of transition it is expressly felt that the old order is yielding place to new. Sensitively when we review the pattern of life in the society, in individual and social counts, we find that there is something lacking in the psychological build-up of the individual which affects his individual and social-self. The psychological built-up likes and dislikes, norms of good and bad, just and unjust, right and wrong, etc. It is reflected in the individual's reactions towards any object, idea, concept, instance or happenings around him. It is a common experience with all of us to conclude that there is no consistency and coherency in the reactions of the individuals when taken individually or collectively on issues of common or social interests. It is surprising at times to find that the educated people behave in a rather disgraceful way than an uneducated man. This social scene general and individual actions in particular make us think that there is lack of conviction and faith in the values of life. This can very well be termed as the crisis of values. The social, religious, political, economic and moral, all these aspects of life in its collective and moral forms are balanced because of certain base and structure of code of conducts. There are certain convictions, don'ts and do's, which if observed, pay in rich dividends so far as the temporal life is concerned. It helps in harmonizing individual and collective self and milk of humanity permeates through all the facets of collective human life. In this sense values are deep conviction and faith in certain facts, ideas, concepts and beliefs, which have stood the test of time. Most of the values are derived from the religious faiths. What religion gives is no other than ethics. The ethical values and religions are coterminous. Spiritual values are of higher order. Value is basically the conviction and faith which is always cherished. Scientific, aesthetic and physical values in the same way differentiate themselves on the grounds of faith and conviction.

The physiological and psychological nature of man provide enough ground for the belief that he has certain needs. Because of these needs and the resultant satisfaction on the fulfilment of these needs, he finds values in such factors as health, character, social justice, skill, art, love, knowledge, philosophy and religion. The values assigned to these are not just subjective feelings, but refer to expressions of these values. These values which reflect themselves in the expressions and experiences of the individuals in social institution are both subjective and objective, human and divine. Such values are the criterion on the basis of which all immediate interests, desires and preferences are appraised.

Human actions can be divided into two types—one, the mechanical and the other intelligent. In the first man will always conceive the movements in a stereotyped way to a narrowly conceived ends. In intelligent actions the component actions are conceived of as variable and adaptable in the light of some generally conceived ends. This requires logic, insight and reasoning on the part of the individual to act in a particular situation. He should not be a subject to pre-established notions. He must be able to judge for himself. He must be aware of his responsibilities and must be ready to make personal choices. Aristotle believed that this rationality can be developed by sound moral habits. Habits formation is a long term activity and needs motivation and inspiration from within and without. Peter R.S. has rightly observed that, "Morality is the correct opinion and conventional behaviour of the well-brought up people. It is a conduct based on the grasp of the fundamental principles." Irving Babbitt and Norman Forester would classify these actions as higher and lower forms of mental processes. As the lower level sensuous appetites, lower imagination, lower will and lower reason account for.

The humanists believe that the powers of the lower nature be subjected to control and direction of the powers of the higher nature. The appetites, impulses and feelings if left uncontrolled and uncultivated, they would destroy both the individual and the civilization. For the development of the integrated individual there is need to organise, harmonise and balance all powers. This is done by self-restraint which is the function of the higher will. The higher will or inner checks set standards which guide or control our actions. This *humanists* believe that any man find within himself a centre that is common to all men. It is the standard of value, the centre of reference in dealing with concrete situations. Then follows *decorum* is the application and in the last *restraint*. Decorum is the application of law of measure, which is imitation of models supplied by higher imagination. The law of measure means cultivation of all the faculties in due proportion. The perfection of the various human capacities requires harmonious development of mental powers. Only conformity to higher standards which the intuitive powers give, man can enjoy true happiness and human welfare.

An integrated personality has a sound base of values. Without values the personality becomes maladjusted. Such an individual will be without any faith and conviction, will not be able to stand against the adversities of life. Values give inner strength and solidarity in action and thought. It helps in forming the philosophy of life. It is, in fact, on the basis of such a philosophy of life that we call any action or reaction as moral or immoral. The judgement of the individual on moral and immoral grounds pertains to his morality. Morality in fact is a high order principle which encompasses all religious preachings and confines in it everything that is best for one and all. It derives its principles from the fundamentals of life stream in the society. These are the same on which the social structure stands. It imbibes culture, heritage, religion and all social institutions. It pertains to the code of conducts in the society. As the society experiences change in its living structures, the code of conducts also get changed. It has happened in the past. Self-realization was the cherished aim of life, the morality of the individuals centred round it. In the age of scientific and technological change, where a new culture is taking place, the morality would have a scientific footing because the new knowledge would give a new meaning and a new definition to the process of life.

The devaluation of values is caused as the value aspect in

the development of personality is neglected. It is due to the deviation from the cultural and philosophical foundations of the society. There also prevails a sort of misunderstanding so far as religious, moral, spiritual, scientific and social values are concerned. Certainly the contents of these values are different to the extent they are confined to those denominations. But when viewed from the general sense the values are one. Conscientiousness or truthfulness are the values common to morality and spirituality. It is equally important in social setting also. The scientific morality of which Emile Durkhiem and R.S. Peter talk of are no other than the moral and social values. Theodore Brameld elaborating his concept of social-self-realization talks of the values which are no other than Durkhiem's or Peter's and terms it as scientific morality. The high order principle of Peter's morality and Durkhiem's morality are virtually the same. The values of different denominations may be labelled differently for convenience but the end and means involved in it are the same. Truthfulness for spiritual ends may have different connotations but the mechanism involved in it and truthfulness for social purpose would be the same.

For value-oriented education it would be the first requirement that the values which are to be developed be defined. It should be decided what we want to make a child a better man, a better citizen, or a better professional man or all combined in one. The frame-work of values would come up from it. As a matter of fact no educational programme is without value-base, it is only that they are not pronounced loudly. Values are neither skills nor piece of knowledge, they are basically faith and conviction. One who has faith in honesty will be honest. One who realised his duty as his religion will always be dutiful and so on. It is something related with the making of the mind and not acquiring something. It is the psychological built-up of the individual. It has to become a way of life. It is only living to the practical things, knowing for oneself and realising the truth one is baptised in values. The greatest values, as talked in our culture, are Truth, Beauty and Love, which can be realised by participating in the art of living.

The art and science, work and philosophy, all that involves the process of living should be so interwoven that the individual realises for himself the bliss of truth, beauty and love. Every piece of art or science is the expression of perfection. It symbolises devotien and determination, thought and expression, sequence and coherence, meaning and purpose. It expresses the union of all the forces of mind and body, emotion and soul, psyche and physique, libido and the id. The works of De Vince and Michelangelo are the true expressions of the realization of the perfect. This could be possible for them by living to the finer vibrations of life around.

To make the values aspect of our educational programmes more prominent, the following curricular and extra-curricular approach seems worth trying. The approaches for primary, secondary ad higher education would be as under.

For primary level the curricular approach would comprise of:

(*a*) In the Language courses such stories and portions could be included which inspire traits like friendliness, sociability, co-operation, etc. While going through these portions the students should be inspired to enact the scenes in the class. Dramatization can be used with the purpose of exposing the particular traits in the character and appealing upon their appreciation.

(*b*) In the social studies too the historical characters of provincial and all India nature be referred to in detail exposing their early childhood, habits and the teachings they were subjected to.

(*c*) In teaching of Geography and Sciences, care should be taken to associate the learner with the nature and society. Observation of the natural phenomenon would inspire them to realise the inherent justice, system, regulation and order, freedom and disciline.

Extra-curricular activities would comprise group and individual activities, team work, working with others, etc. Observation trips, visits to social institutions, public places etc. readings from books, sermons by teachers, writing of quotes, preparation of poster, etc., are some of the activities which can be taken up. Insistence on assembly, attendance and going out of the class, appreciation of the good conduct of the students and its recognition are some other ways to make students realise that good acts and habits distinguish them from others. There dawns a feeling of superiority and they feel encouraged.

The programmes for the Secondary level would also include the above but would have a broader footing and wider coverage. The curricular approach would be, besides the inclusion of topics, to stimulate values, cover such portions from different literature and religions that could be cited side by side of our own. Language, social sciences, natural and physical sciences would be taught with making room for and utilizing occasions for references of the matter outside the text. Care would be taken to expose the values of the subjects, for each subject has its own value, relating and emphasising its importance to human life. Teaching of language provides very many occasions to fall upon the appeal to inculcate the healthy attitudes. The extra-curricular programmes would again have a wider coverage. Thought for the day-type activities can be introduced, where the students, would be asked to collect thoughts from different sources and discuss it in the class. Before or at the end of the school day reading by the students on any one value be organised. At the time of assembly talks by the teachers, of short duration, can be organised. Readings from sacred literature from different religions can be held. Incentives for proper behaviour and habits be given. Commendation and colours of the school be given in the general function especially organised in the school. School volunteer corps on the lines of scouts be established and students in batches be sent for social services. The mela-duty, Bazar-duty, scarcity-relief work, etc., are other activities which shall develop in them the spirit of co-operation, sacrifice, duty, sympathy, tolerance, helpfulness and many more.

At the higher stage curricular approach would be too complicated. Extra-curricular activities can be meaningful. Introduction of comparative religion, ethics and morality as a special paper can be introduced at the under-graduate level. It should be made compulsory at the under-graduate level for the students to participate in the developmental projects going on in the country. For this there should be regular recruitment of students in the University Voluntary Force and in every vacation they be sent in batches or rather assigned areas and work to do. The NSS and NCC wings in the Universities and take up these programmes. Better if the students are sent to different parts of the country and engaged in different projects going on. They should be provided lodging and boarding facilities free of charge and paid pocket money. In return they would be performing works like literacy classes, health and sanitation, general awareness, agriculture and many related things, supervision of many project works. This will give them first hand knowledge of the people and the land and emotionally attach them to various developmental programmes, for they have put their sweat and toil in the completion of it. It shall give them pride and a sense of oneness. Physically associating young people to works enlightens them to the charm of working and creating something. Sweating together and toiling for the common end inspires finer feelings in the fellow-workers. This would be in true sense developing national consciousness, which in itself is the greatest value so far as social-self-realization is concerned. The unions in the college and universities can be encouraged to take up such social work as distribution of ration, controlling of the traffic in the towns, checking the ticketless passengers, helping police and home-guards in maintaining law and order, providing information of anti-social purpose but also make them conscious of their shortcomings in habits and behaviour, ultimately leading them to imbibe basic values of life. This will also help in solving indiscipline problems in institutions.

With the above our examination system also needs reform. We all know that the academic value of it is already lost and the utilitarian value is also diminishing. The provision in the NEP (1986) of delinking degrees and diplomas with employment is on the right lines. Let there be examinations conducted by the recruiting and employing agencies and bodies. This will save the present generation from demoralization. If only qualities of head and heart, habits and manners are given equal weightage with the degrees and diplomas, the value aspect of our education will be revived again.

REFERENCES

1. Babbit Irving—On Being Creative, Boston, 1932.
2. Bais, H.S. Education in Values, Teacher To-day, 1982.
3. Bantock, G.H.—Education and Values, Faber & Faber, London, 1965.
4. Brightman, E.S.—An Introduction to Philosophy, N.Y. Holt, 1953.
5. Dahlke Otto, H.—Values in Culture and Classroom, Harper, N.Y. 58.
6. Forester Norman—Humanism and American, N. Y. Reinhart, 1930.
7. Horne, H.H.—Philosophies of Education, National Society for the Study of Education, Chicago, 1942.
8. Hutchins, R.M.—Education for Freedom, Baton Rouge, 1943.
9. Peter, R.S.—Authority, Respect and Education, George Allen, London.

23
Role of Values in Teacher Effectiveness

Manoj Kumar Saxena, B.R. Kukreti
Sandhya Gihar

The all pervasive violence, brutality, apathy and lack of understanding that we see around us are the outcomes of a valueless society. Majority of man can, to any extent, to achieve power and wealth, the two ultimate destination in the present age. This is because of the total neglect of the process of inculcating values in our schools and colleges. Because of such a school environment the students are losing the purpose of life and they fail to distinguish between appearance and reality. In our educational institutions on certain occasions preaching of values is done but the "values cannot be promoted by repeating words". They need effective teachers who themselves are value oriented. It is our everyday experience to observe that children imitate their teachers not in words but in their behaviour. Teachers play a very significant role in inculcating values in children. The teachers' role in the total educational process is vital, as child's behaviour, attitude, interest, etc. are greatly influenced by teachers (Gupta, 2001)

In order to inculcate values in the students, the primary requirement is that he/she should have natural value fixation in him/her. Once a teacher's behaviour becomes value oriented, his power to influence the child increases resulting in a tremendous increase in his effectiveness. Today the erosion of values and all-pervading cynicism in the society has made it all the more obligatory to focus our attention on values. It is the teacher who can become the catalytic agent for imbibing the values among students and they should get ready to face the challenges on slaught of value devaluation being carried out by the modern society and modern media. It has become essential that a teacher in order to become more effective should increase the role of value in his/her life.

It is imperative because the prosperity and development of our country does not depend only on the materialistic aspect but it can be assessed through the ideal characteristics of the citizen. Education plays a prominent role in the creation of good citizen. Formation of good citizens depends on the quality of teachers. The value orientation of teachers has a great effect on his man-making process. Education can succeed in process of man making only if the teachers are effective, because it is a teacher who is the real dynamic force in the institution behind all the educational activities.

The significance of the teacher in the society cannot be denied he is a friend, guide and philosopher imbibing in him noble cultural traditions (Dropkin, 1967), custodian of the future (Gandhi, 1970), sainted pioneer of civilization and moving force behind social, economic and cultural advancement (Page, 1971). He is so powerful that he can stimulate the changing process of the society in right direction. We can, therefore, conclude that the role of teacher in the process of education is unquestionable. No educational system can drive without the help of cultured and competent teacher. An efficient successful teacher is an unavoidable factor in educational improvement. Knowledge is not enough for making a teacher effective and successful. Formal interview and an academic achievement generally do not provide effective teacher. Teachers so selected fail to control the clean, many of them cannot satisfy the students. As such, in addition to this academic record, the selection authority should put emphasis on the value education. The necessary quality and characteristic of a candidate to be selected as a teacher.

Some investigation have been conducted to find out the relationship between teaching effectiveness and value pattern of teachers, Koul (1972) made an attempt to sort out the differentiating sprangerian values of popular and non-popular teachers. The study revealed that popular teachers were significantly high on theoretical, social and religious values than non-popular ones. Chandra (1977) has found that effective teachers were obtained significantly higher scores on social value and knowledge value. Singh (1978) had studied the relationship between economic value and teaching success and found a negative relationship between these two variables. Mutha (1980) has also reported that religious, social, theoretical, aesthetic, economic and political values, significantly predicted to teacher effectiveness. Kumar (1985) has also made an attempt to study the relationship of teacher effectiveness with value pattern. This study indicated that ineffective teachers got higher scores on political value. Rajput (2000) remarked that values of kindness character achieving the ideal service to humanity, fearlessness, purity in personal life, freedom from just and quest for truth have been lost somewhere in the search of materialistic gains.

Thus, from the above review it can be admitted that the findings related to values pattern and success in teaching are neither conclusive nor consistent. To obtain somewhat more definite results in the present study an effort has been made to study the role values in teacher effectiveness.

Objectives of the Study:

Present investigation has aimed at the following objectives:

1. To study the value pattern of the effective & ineffective teachers.
2. To study the value pattern of effective and ineffective teachers in respect to their sex.
3. To suggest how appropriate values can inculcate in teachers to make them effective.

Sample and Sampling Technique:

In the present investigation multistage random sampling technique was adopted to draw the sample. At the first stage, 15 secondary schools were chosen randomly from the population of 48 secondary schools of Banswara district of Rajasthan. Keeping in view the sexwise representation of teachers in the sample, 300 teachers were selected randomly from these 15 sample schools at second phase of sample selection. Then teacher efficiency scale (TES) was administered on these selected teachers. Teacher efficiency scale (TES) is developed and standardized by N.S. Chauhan and R. Jain (1976). At the initial stage with the help of median, the 300 sample subjects were categories ineffective teachers (above median point 289.5) and ineffective teachers (below median point 289.5) by analysing the teacher efficiency score. Both the groups of teachers (effective N = 179 and ineffective N = 121) were further categorised into male and female categories. In order to understand the effect of value pattern on the level of success of teaching 't' test were used. In order to be able to know the value pattern of the teachers eight value scale (EVS) developed and standardized by Prof. Beena Shah (1986) was used.

Tool:

For the purpose of data collection, in the present study following tools were-used :

1. Teacher efficiency scale (TES) developed and standardized by N.S. Chauhan and R. Jain, 1976.
2. Eight value scale (EVS) developed and standardized by Prof. Beena Shah, 1986.

TES has 110 items distributed into three categories - A, B, C category. 'A' refers to presage criteria with 83 items, category 'B' refers to the process criteria with 15 items and category 'A' and 'B' judges are the students and items are open to 4 students to appraisal to a particular teacher. The category 'C' for the teacher to whom students appraised to make appraisal of the students growth.

EVS consists of 32 items each followed by three placesible. It is a forced choice type scale. It is measured eight values, namely Knowledge, Economic, Aesthetic, Social, Political, Religious, Creative, Humanistic.

Result and Discussion:

TABLE 1
Mean and S.D. scores of effective teachers (ET) and ineffective teachers (IT) on different values.

Sl. No.	Values	Mean ET (N = 179)	Mean IT (N = 121)	S.D. ET (N = 179)	S.D. IT (N = 121)	't' value
1.	Knowledge value	27.60	22.13	4.21	4.96	14.41*
2.	Economic value	23.44	27.55	5.01	3.94	11.06*
3.	Aesthetic value	22.04	22.54	4.08	3.65	1.56*
4.	Social value	24.17	24.37	2.91	3.82	0.71*
5.	Political value	20.89	25.60	4.45	5.32	11.64*
6.	Religious value	24.17	23.62	3.78	3.58	1.81*
7.	Creative value	25.42	22.77	4.03	4.83	7.22*
8.	Humanistic value	25.47	24.18	5.17	4.24	3.31*

*Significant at .01 level of significance·· Significant at. 05 level of significance.

An examination of table-1 shows that effective teachers possess higher knowledge value than their ineffective counterparts (t = 14.41, p = .01). On the dimension of economic value, again a significant variation was obtained between both groups of comparison effective and ineffective teachers. It concludes that a negative relationship exists between economic value and teaching effectiveness. Both the groups were found almost similar on aesthetic dimension (t = 1.56, n.s). Above table presents an insignificant variation on mean social values scores of teacher belonging to effective and ineffective groups (t = .76, n.s). Thus, this concludes that social value may not be considered as an important determinant of effective teaching. Ineffective teachers had scored higher mean value than effective teachers on political dimension. On religious value no significant difference was found between effective and ineffective teachers (t = 1.81, n.s.). The mean of creative value score of effective teachers were comparatively higher than those of ineffective ones (t = 7.22, p = .01). Effective teachers have significantly higher humanistic value than their ineffective colleagues (t = 3.31, p = .01).

TABLE 2
Mean and S.D. scores of effective male teachers (EMT) and ineffective male teachers (IMT) on different values.

Sl. No.	Values	Mean EMT (N = 102)	Mean IMT (N = 78)	S.D. EMT (N = 102)	S.D. IMT (N = 78)	't' value
1.	Knowledge value	27.28	22.50	4.47	3.84	10.28**
2.	Economic value	24.48	27.12	4.75	3.98	9.46**
3.	Aesthetic value	21.53	22.37	4.27	3.55	1.92
4.	Social value	24.29	24.38	3.10	5.10	0.20
5.	Political value	21.98	25.82	4.85	5.16	6.89**
6.	Religious value	24.26	23.99	3.47	3.70	0.67
7.	Creative value	25.17	22.81	4.49	5.67	4.17**
8.	Humanistic value	25.33	24.10	5.36	4.34	2.26**

Significant at 0.1 level of significance Significant at .015 level of significance.

In case of male teachers, as shown in table-2 reveals a significant and positive relationship were found among the variable of success in teaching and knowledge value (t = 10.28, p = .01), Creative value (t = 4.17, p = .01) and Humanistic value (t = 2.26, p = .05). In respect of social value no significant variation was found between effective and ineffective male teachers. Both effective male teachers and ineffective male teachers reveal significant but negative association on political dimension of value scale (t = 6.89, p = .01). Religious value score shows negligible difference between effective and ineffective teachers. Unsuccessful group of male teachers were found to have higher economic value than the successful group of male teachers (t = 9.46, p = .01). No significant difference was found to exist between the mean score of effective and ineffective teachers on Aesthetic value (t = 1.92, n.s.).

TABLE 3

Mean and S.D. scores of effective female teachers (EFT) and ineffective female teachers (IFT) on different values.

Sl. No.	Values	Mean EFT (N = 77)	Mean IFT (N = 43)	S.D. EFT (N = 77)	S.D. IFT (N = 43)	't' value
1.	Knowledge value	27.94	21.64	4.00	6.12	9.84··
2.	Economic value	22.29	28.14	5.38	3.98	10.16··
3.	Aesthetic value	22.62	22.78	3.93	3.81	0.33
4.	Social value	24.10	24.36	2.93	2.62	0.78
5.	Political value	19.64	25.31	4.15	5.57	9.33··
6.	Religious value	24.07	23.14	4.16	3.45	1.99··
7.	Creative value	25.71	22.74	3.67	3.79	6.50··
8.	Humanistic value	25.64	24.29	5.13	4.21	2.35··

··Significant at .01 level of significance ·Significant at .05 level of significance.

Above Table 3 shows the same result as found in case of male teachers. It means success of teaching is effected by knowledge, creative and Humanistic value. Effective female teachers have significantly higher knowledge value as compared to ineffective female teachers (t = 9.84, p = .01). Comparison of effective female teachers and ineffective female teachers shows that ineffective female teachers had higher economic value than effective female teachers (t = 10.16, p = .01). No significant difference was found on aesthetic value score (t = .33, n.s.). Both effective female teachers and ineffective female teachers have almost similar on social value (t = .78, n.s.). There seems to exist a significant difference between the effective female teachers and ineffective female teachers on political value, for the ineffective female teachers was found to have higher mean score than effective female teachers on this value (t = 9.33, p = 0.01). The above table leads us to the conclusion that religiousity makes no difference on the level of teacher effectiveness in teaching. Both female teachers have same mean score on this dimension. Comparatively higher mean scores were obtained in case of successful female teachers have the same mean score on the same dimension. Comparatively higher mean scores were obtained in case of effective female teachers than their ineffective counterparts on creative and humanistic dimension of value scale (t = 6.5, p = .01 and t = 2.35, p = .01).

On the basis of the above discussion the following findings may be concluded :

(1) In the prediction of effective and ineffective teachers' knowledge, creative and humanistic values play dominating role in making a teacher effective. It is natural that the teacher who possesses the dominant interest in advancement of knowledge by an empirical, critical, rational and intellectual approach having favourable attitude towards higher academic achievement, interest in discovery of new innovations may create a favourable atmosphere in the classroom by providing to students upto date knowledge of the subject.

(2) Higher humanistic value among the effective teachers develop better student teacher relationship. The teacher gives proper attention to the children having poor reading learning ability. So, humanistic behaviour increases the effectiveness of the teacher. Thus, all students show their liking towards such teachers.

(3) On economic and political value ineffective teachers had scored significantly higher mean value than effective teachers. The teacher have developed earning attitude in the field of education, naturally their changed attitude has diminished the effectiveness of teacher. A person who joins this vocation due to well-paid salary will not be sincere towards his profession.

(4) Further on controlling sex (male/female), when these two groups (effective and ineffective) of teachers were composed on different values, the effective teachers have revealed similar value pattern as found earlier in case of total teachers (i.e. strong knowledge, creative and humanistic values and weak economic and political values). Except on religious and humanistic values. Whereas effective female teachers have shown more inclination towards religious activities in comparison to their ineffective counterparts. The reason of high religious value of effective female teachers may be because the teachers who possess faith in divine power and religion and who engage themselves in rituals related to religion they may

be more responsible and devoted to their work.

Cultivating Values Among Teachers:

It is well known that the right discipline is an institution consists not in external compulsion but in healthy moral influence and habits of the mind which lead spontaneously to desired behaviour (Khandelwal, 2001). For acceptance of values one has to willingly deal with adopt the values as a basis of human behaviour and guiding force in our life. Accepting the importance of value in life, educational efforts should be directed for:

1. Acquisition initiation of values.
2. Values sustenance and continuity.
3. Value change and modification, and
4. Value integration (Sudhir, 2001).

In order to inculcate values in teachers by the institutions the acquisition, sustenance, modification and integration strategies have to be planned and implemented. Initiation for value development the teacher requires a congenial environment to be created. The teacher's self/concept has to be transformed into a positive personality. His ideal images need sublimation of finer sentiments and prejudices with negative direction have to be erased.

Another way is to expose the teacher to useful association and conditions causing satisfaction and enjoyment. Value study groups, environmental study groups, mercy to animal group, social and cultural groups, science and life group can be formed and free discussion can provide very good reinforcement to value inculcation among teachers. In these discussion forums the teachers would get an opportunity of expressing their thoughts and feeling along with their view-points. The authorities have to be sympathetic towards their problems. There may be grievances, but a healthy communication and objective evaluation shall lead to formation and propagation of values.

Along with discussion the weekly extension lectures containing the moral and ethical values can also be arranged. Such lectures can deal with significant value content in the light of existing modern situation.

The institutions can also arrange periods for internal meditation and scanning one's behaviour in the light of desired values. Such self-evaluation can bring change in the overt behaviour of a teacher, inculcating in him desired values. This is known as internalizing the values. The values become the part of the psyche and evolve ego ideals. This process involves imitation, identification, internalization, sublimation and projection. This process will help not only information but also the sustenance of the values.

Through the role play technique teacher may prepare briefing, explaining the situation and evaluating his performance through constructed evaluation. The institution should also try to help the teacher in overcoming his anxiety and where sensitive issues are concerned, should proceed and try to divert the mind of the teacher to positive direction giving him happy experience.

Institution can also adopt "Skinner Shaping Technique", fixed action programmes having proper attitudes towards values can be prepared and implemented which teachers can practice and group performances should be rewarded. For this purpose the institution can prepare task groups freedom should be given to teachers selecting the task, designing activities and accepting their roles and responsibilities.

Students like good, loving and parent like behaviour in a teacher, one who is not rude and does not use offending language, Impartiality and absence of discrimination are other attributes expected from a teacher. For becoming effective he has to be regular and punctual. All such habits and qualities occur out of humanistic values, not merely the knowledge of subject content but also the about good manners, latest developments, moral education, good books, positive thinking and good 'Sanskar' with in order to become an effective teacher or an institution to make its teacher effective, it has to plan strategies for the inculcation of the values, i.e. social knowledge, creative, aesthetic and humanistic values. The most harming and alarming values rendering a teacher ineffective are economic and political values which need to be eradicated. The humanistic values like patriotism, honesty, dignity of labour, courage and straight forwardness. Along with the strategies suggested in this paper strategies like values clarification, critical thinking exercises, articulation of value positions, developing sense of duty, etc. should also be adopted.

As the study indicates that the majority of effective teachers as against ineffective ones were found to have high knowledge, creative and humanistic values and low political and economic values. It seems reasonable, therefore, to recommend that in teachers training programmes and in its syllabus, these modifications should be done, which develop the advancement of knowledge by an empirical, critical, rational and intellectual approach, favourable attitude towards higher academic achievement, originality in thought, interest in the discovery of new innovations, love for science and technology, devotion to render his service to the students, love and respect for his pupils, colleagues and society, enthusiasm to enhance his status in the college as well as in the society. On the other hand such chapters should be added in the syllabus, which will diminish the materialistic feelings, attitude towards industrialists and business related matters and thrust of money and material gain through his profession.

REFERENCES

Drokin, S. Teaching in transitions, The Queen's College Review, The City University of New York, pp. 3-8, 1967.

Gandhi, Indira, Tributes of teachers, Northern India Patrika, 19, 7, page 5, 1970.

Gupta, M.S., Personal and professional values of an effective teacher student's perception, Journal of value education, NCERT, No. 2, Page-98, July 2001.

Koul, S., Personality factors, values and interest among the most accepted and least accepted secondary school female teachers of Mathura district, Ph.D. Psy., Agra University, 1997.

Khandelwal, B.P., Values for human excellence, Journal of value education, NCERT, Vol. 1, No. 1, Page 124, Jan. 2001.

Kumar, P., Teacher effectiveness as related with value orientation at secondary level teaching, Journal of education and Psychology, Vol. XXXX III, No. 1, pp. 22.26, 1985.

Mutha, D.N., An attitudinal and personality study of effective teachers, Ph.D. Psy., Jodhpur University, 1980.

Page, A.D., Teacher : A neglected class, Phi Delta Kappan, 36, 6, pp. 81-97, 1971.

Rajput, J.S., Cuture and community—putting 'spirit' back into education, New Delhi : The Times of India 18 August, 2000.

Singh, A., "Self Concept of Teachers and their emotional adjustment". Ph.D. thesis, education, M.D. University, Rohtak, pp. 72-76, 1978.

Singh, A., et.al., Inculcation of values at secondary stage, Journal of value education, NCERT, Vol. 1, No. 1, pp. 45-49, January 2001.

Sudhir, M.A., Human values strategies for development, Journal of value education, NCERT, Vol. 1, No. 2, pp. 26-30, July 2001.

24
Education and Human Value

Bhopal Singh
Shireesh Pal Singh

Society is shaped by the prevailing system of education.Needed changes in a society are the outcomes of education provided to its citizens. Education is the basic requirement for the survival and proliferation of democracy.The key stone of democracy conceived is education, not only education that is accessible to all, but education whose aims and methods have been throughout afresh. Learning is gained through experiences and for efficient learning education is necessary. When we talk of giving education to our young ones, we means that such experiences are provided to them which may help them to grow individually, physically, mentally, morally, spiritually and emotionally.

Education is a purposeful social process of a society which helps to develop the innate power of a human being and it also develop its mental level, education level and brings a drastic change in human behaviour. It is education, only which makes a men civilized, cultured and true citizen of country.

Value education is ingrained in every tradition of Indian culture. Yet it is a matter of regret that gradually we are losing our values with the result that we tend to become corrupt and hypocrite. This trend must be checked urgently. Perhaps a major responsibility for the correctives action lies on our leaders in different walks of life. Nevertheless educational institutions can also play a significant role in the promotion of values.

Meaning of the Term Value

In the word of John Dewey, "Value means primarily to prize, to esteem, to appraise, to estimate; to means the act of cherising something, holding it dear and also the act of passing judgement upon the nature and amounts of values as compared with something else." A value stands for ideas men live for. They are the part and parcel of the philosophy of a nation and that of its educational system. They are the guiding principles of life.

Need of Value Education

The following are some reasons that may be mentioned in this connection:

1. The progress in science and technology without simultaneous development of moral values could have serious in many areas of life. It is very essential that moral awareness is promoted to orient the progress in science and technology towards the welfare of mankind.
2. With the general decline of traditional values, some common values should be rediscovered to unite human beings.
3. Schools can remain hardly neutral so far value education is concerned. Teachers are always passing on some values to their students whether they are conscious of it or not through their conduct in and out of classroom, through there selection of books to be read through their choice of instructional strategies and so on.
4. So there is a need for a consciously planned value education prgramme in schools curriculum.
5. There is an increasing moral complexity in the contemporary world and pupils are expected to face more complicated decision making situations about issues involving values. They should be help in developing the ability to make proper choices in such situations.

6. It can not be ignored that the rate of juvenile and delinquency is increasing everywhere. It is a definite symptoms of a crises which todays youth undergoes in the process of is personal both. In such a situations values education assumes a special significance.

Inculcation of Values

Value education is not a one shot,unitary type of process. School and teachers should have their significant contribution towards value education. For value orientated education it would be the first requirement that the value which are to be develop to be defined clearly. It should be decided that we want to make a child a better man, a better citizen or a better allrounder.The teacher has to take special interest and care in providing learning experiences of different types to integrate value into the content.In actual learning both the learning experiences and content are in constant interaction. Some of the Human values which has to be develop in a child for being a good citizen are as follows:

1. Responsibility.
2. Honesty.
3. Love.
4. Respect.
5. Humanity.
6. Tolerance.
7. Unity.
8. Co-operation.
9. Peace.
10. Simplicity

- School Principal and teachers can organize these activities to inculcate the values in the students:
- **Morning Assembly:** Through this activity, students gain the values of orderliness and punctuality.
- **Flag Hoisting:** Devotion, peace, team spirit can be developed by this activity.
- **Cultural Programmes:** Co-operation, good manners and sense of responsibility becomes organized this activity.
- **Group Games and Sports:** Co-operation, Consideration

for others, Sense of responsibility, love and respect of rules can be developed by these activities.

- **Celebration of National Days:** National Spirit and Patriotism can be developed by this activity.
- **School Cleanliness:** Love for cleanliness and dignity of labour developed in students by this activity.
- **Social Service Camps:** Love for loyalty, dignity of labour and selfless spirit becomes through this activity.

REFERENCES

Bhat, R.K., (1996), Towards a Value Based Education System, University News,Vol. xiv, No. 43, pp. 9-10.

Gupta, N.L., *Human Value in Education*, New Delhi, Concept Publishing Company.

Mohanty, A., Integration of Human Value in Teacher Education, University Education, Vol. 41, No. 34, Aug. 2003.